THE
UNDERTAKER'S
DAUGHTER

—— A Daughter's Tribute ——

TRACEY VAN DER VEER

In loving memory of my darling father
21/10/1943 to 24/06/2024
The man I was privileged to call my dad.

ACKNOWLEDGEMENTS

To my mum and sister I thank you for everything. I would not have gotten through the hardest time of my life without you. I never wanted to be on this devastating journey, but I'm glad I got to do it with you. We really did do dad proud.

Thank you to my beautiful children for your support. You lost your grandad, but you never lost sight that I was losing my dad. You and your children give me the strength to carry on.

I thank my brother in law, Mark, for always being there when we all needed you. You are the brother I never had.

Thank you to my incredible husband. Always there for me, believing in me and ready to catch me when I fall. You allowed me to give my father the best last months of his life and for that, I am eternally grateful.

Thank you to Father Morgan. A true friend to my dad until the end.

I am eternally grateful to all of the hospital and hospice team.

I would like to give thanks to the family and friends who helped me on my devastating journey of grief. Your support, kind words and help will never be forgotten. You were collectively my lighthouse in a terrifying storm.

Lastly, I give thanks to my dad. There are no words to describe my gratitude.

CONTENTS

SYNOPSIS

Tracey is the daughter of a retired undertaker, Leslie, a funny man who laughed more at his own jokes than anyone else. Leslie had provided well for his family, but his job was not an easy one. Taking work home with him literally and metaphorically was all part of every day life for Tracey and her family whilst growing up.

A call out of the blue one evening from her mum brought her world crashing down. Leslie was suddenly rushed into hospital and this was to be the beginning of the end.

Tracey had to leave her home and husband Rob in Spain to be with her father, mother Sue and sister Hayley, who needed her the most. The many weeks that followed were the hardest of her life. Weeks filled with heartache, sadness, happiness and tears. The making of new memories was crucial in finding a way forward to accepting a life without the most important member of their family. The tears flowed, they did not stop. She knew they never would.

The weeks spent in the hospital, the hospice and at the family home were to be the hardest life journey Tracey had to make. Ensuring that every moment was spent making her father feel comfortable, happy and, above all, loved. Making the sacrifice to be away from her husband and home to be there for her family. The ultimate gift she could give her dad was to be there for him when he needed her the most.

You would think that being an undertaker's daughter would help when faced with circumstances like these, but how wrong was she? From the request not to be resuscitated to inviting the vicar for tea and all the things in between. This was going to be one hell of a ride, and she was not prepared for it.

Cherished childhood memories were revisited and new memories were created. The roller coaster of emotions was heartbreaking. Tears became laughter and laughter became tears. Tracey and her family were there until the bitter end when Leslie took his last breath.

Life after Leslie's departure became eventful when signs appeared showing that he was still around. Sue decided to sell the family home to live with Hayley and Tracey had to move on with her life. A life that would never be the same again.

THE BEGINNING OF THE END

"Pause the movie please, Rob, Mum's video calling." Rob paused the Netflix movie so that I could answer Mum's call. We regularly had a WhatsApp video call, so nothing seemed out of the ordinary. There was Mum crying her eyes out, crying so much that she could barely speak. "Rob, quick, come here. Mum is in a terrible state."

After several minutes of trying to calm Mum down, she was finally able to tell us what was wrong. "Dad has been rushed into hospital, we are here now waiting to know what is happening," she said. I was unable to respond, panic took hold of me and the shock was like a punch in the guts. I felt totally winded. Dad was never unwell, so this was a complete bolt out of the blue. Now, living in Spain is not that far away, but when emergencies happen, it makes you feel like you are on the other side of the world... I might as well have been because my dad was there and needed me. How helpless did I feel...? I felt bloody useless.

Hayley took the phone from Mum. She was in shock, too. She explained that she and her husband had been on their annual holiday to Cornwall and decided to have a day trip to Devon to surprise Mum and Dad. Thank god they did. Dad was writhing in agony when they arrived. We have never known Dad to complain about aches and pains or to make visits to the doctor, so if he said he was in pain, it had to be very serious. My sister had ignored Dad's protests not to call an ambulance because, of course, it was evident that he needed medical attention fast. The ambulance crew arrived, and after a few tests, he was blue-lighted to hospital. They would be staying there with Mum and would keep us updated. "I had better get off the phone, sis. I need to book some flights." I hung up the phone, shaking like a leaf. "Rob, I need to get flights home as soon as possible."

I switched on the laptop and prayed I would find a flight to get home fast. The laptop screen was all blurry from all my crying, and I could hardly type as I was shaking uncontrollably. Now, someone was definitely looking out for me because I managed to find a flight leaving very early the following morning. The flight was booked, some clothes were thrown in a bag, and then I had a very long, sleepless night. I watched every second of that clock tick by throughout the night, worried sick that I would miss my flight. Morning eventually came, and Rob took me to the airport. The two hours before boarding seemed like an eternity, but eventually, I boarded the flight and made my way home. My cousin and his wife were waiting for me at the airport arrivals. They had heard what had happened and were not going to let me waste any more time getting to my dad. There they were with a coffee for me, and we raced back to their car to make the two-hour journey to the hospital. I was so grateful for their kindness. I will always remember what they did for me. Little did I know it then, but their kindness was something I was going to rely on a lot in the coming months. The two-hour car journey seemed to go on forever. My tears were streaming down my face. I felt sick. What was I going to do?

I swung in through the hospital doors and made my way to the elevator and up to the ward. Dad was not expecting to see me there. We had a very emotional reunion. "You shouldn't have come home. I'm okay," he said. It was typical of him to play things down so as not to worry us more. Of course, I was going to be there; my dad needed me, and I would not have wanted to be anywhere else. My priority became my dad, and, of course, my mum and my sister needed my support. Dad was waiting to be taken to the theatre to find out the problem. He had several scans and tests during the night, and he was told that he would need emergency surgery. The scans had identified a lump, so the operation was necessary.

Mum, Hayley and I watched Dad helplessly as he was wheeled away to be prepped for surgery. He waved us off. I just couldn't bear it. I collapsed in the corridor in a heap. I was the strong one, or was I? Mum suggested that we go to the café to have a cup of tea, so I composed myself and off we went. We had an agonizing wait of over five hours, and eventually, Mum got the call from the nurse to say that Dad was due out of recovery and would soon be back to the ward. We made our way back to the ward and there was Dad, as bright as a button, looking very pleased with himself. We later decided to go back home whilst Dad got a good night's sleep. We all hugged Dad tearfully and said we would be back the next morning.

Morning eventually came, and we made our way to the hospital. Dad was sitting up in bed and very calmly explained that the doctor was going to see us and explain everything in detail. He told us they were going to operate. "I will be okay," he said. I wish that had been true because if it were, our selfless, lovely dad would still be with us. We chatted away, trying to be as normal as possible whilst waiting for the doctor to do his rounds. The doctor arrived and explained that he wanted to speak to all of us privately so that he could explain everything and answer any questions we had.

We were taken to a family room and sat there in total shock, dreading the news that was to follow. The doctor explained that Dad had stage four bowel cancer and that the cancer had metastasized to his liver. The news was delivered in a very factual manner, it was hard to take it all in. A nurse was present and then suddenly, we saw it—a green folder—a McMillan folder.

Reality fell upon us like a ton of bricks. My dad had cancer. The green folder brimming with leaflets offering support was handed to Dad. He took the folder, the light had gone from his eyes. It was obvious that he was holding it all together for us. Hearing the doctor's words was one thing, but seeing that folder was the reality, staring us all in the face. He never opened that folder, not once. Now, Dad was not in denial but wanted to put his total trust in the medical team that literally held his life in their hands. I held it together as long as I could, but hearing the cold, hard facts and discovering my dad had the dreaded "C" was more than I could bear. Huge heaving sobs and a tsunami of grief washed over me. I was drowning in sorrow and did not know how to deal with it. There we were in this small room, all crying, and Dad held it all together, trying to comfort us. Why was this happening to my lovely dad?

"I'll be okay," Dad assured us. He wasn't

okay, but we hoped he would be.

I sat in that room, feeling like the walls were closing in on me whilst the plan of action was discussed. Dad was to undergo an operation to fit a temporary Stoma and once his infection was under control, he could have his operation and a course of chemotherapy to try to shrink the tumors. After a few days, Dad was discharged from the hospital and sent home. I stayed with my family for a few extra days, then had to return home to Rob and my business. I did not want to go, but I knew, at that point, I had to. A few weeks later, Mum called to update us that Dad's operation date had been set. There I was, booking more flights so that I could be there at every stage with my lovely family.

The day soon arrived, and we all went to the hospital with Dad, and we again had an agonizing wait in the café whilst Dad went for his operation. I would have given anything to have taken his place. Dad literally sailed through his operation to have his Stoma and was very soon after back to his ward telling his jokes to anyone who would listen. I had heard all of his jokes repeatedly throughout my life and I used to tell people not to laugh because he would go on and on telling loads more! I would give anything to hear his jokes now. I miss them so much. After a few days, he was back at home to recover from his surgery. He very quickly adapted to his new way of life, making light of everything. He had regular appointments with the Stoma team, and they helped him immensely. They actually became like part of the family and Dad loved their visits. The weeks passed by, and then it was time for Dad's chemo to start.

Mum, my sister and I followed Dad into the hospital waiting room. Dad looked like a rabbit caught in the headlights as we sat in the waiting room, waiting for his name to be called. The reality was setting in. Dad's having chemo.

Mum went in with Dad, and my sister and I sat

patiently waiting for what seemed like hours whilst Dad was receiving his first treatment. Out, he came looking so pleased with himself. My brave dad made it look like a walk in the park. Only three more sessions to go and then more tests to see if the treatment was working. Thankfully, there were no nasty side effects like sickness or hair loss. He had the colour back in his cheeks and a huge appetite, so we naturally assumed he was getting better. The day before each round of Chemo, blood tests were done to make sure that Dad could have the next treatment. We actually were all told that certain markers in the blood tests had indicated that he was responding well to his treatment... what a relief... A short-lived relief.

Dad's scans were scheduled, and then the agonising wait for the results. We were all invited to meet the surgeon. He was a very nice Italian man with the most calming manner. We were ushered into his small office and there we all sat, waiting for the results of the scans. "I'm sorry, the chemo hasn't worked, and the cancer is spreading." Our world stopped turning. The shock was paralysing. Why was this happening? We had such high hopes that the treatment was working. Even worse was that we were told that the cancer had spread to the channel between the bladder and the bowel.

"What options do I have?" asked Dad. The surgeon gave Dad his options, which included doing nothing. That was not an option for Dad. He was fighting it all the way. Dad opted for a complicated surgery to remove some of the cancer. This was not a cure but a means of potentially buying some time. Dad didn't want to leave us, he wasn't giving up without a fight. We did say that we would support whatever decision he made, but ultimately, it had to be his choice. We did not want him going through any more surgery just for us.

The surgery was scheduled for a few weeks

later, and once again, we made our way to the hospital. Dad was led in like a lamb to slaughter. "I'm okay, I'll see you soon," he said. Me, Mum and my sister spent the many hours that followed in a complete daze. The clock seemed to tick slower and slower. Several coffees later, Mum got the call to say that Dad was in recovery and we could see him soon. We were at Dad's bedside as soon as he was in the ward, and he was surprisingly bright considering his ordeal. "The operation was a success," he said cheerfully. We all cried tears of relief. Those tears soon turned into tears of devastation. That afternoon, the surgeon came to see us and update us on Dad's surgery. The blue curtains were drawn around the bed for privacy. We were told that he had tried his best but could not remove the tumors and that there was nothing more they could do. More tears. Where did they come from? I was crying rivers. "Please do not resuscitate me," Dad blurted out. We all sat there completely dumbfounded. "There would be no point," he said. He explained that he had endured more than enough. The Doctor went off to retrieve the paperwork for Dad to sign. There in bold red letters DO NOT RESUSCITATE. We watched him sign that paperwork without any hesitation. A board was placed on the wall behind his bed and he pointed that board out to every new medical person that came to his aid from that day onwards.

Dad was told he'd be in hospital for up to five days and then would be sent home to recover from his invasive surgery. When he was strong enough, there was a possibility of having radiotherapy to buy him a little more time. Did Dad dream his surgery was successful? Maybe it was wishful thinking, or just maybe Dad couldn't deliver the news himself to the people he loved the most in the world.

You'd think growing up all your life with a Funeral Director Dad, you'd be prepared.

Nothing could have prepared me for this heartbreaking situation. I just thought that my kind, funny dad would live forever. How wrong I was!

He was stapled down the centre of his stomach, it looked like a zip. Drips, heart monitors, oxygen and the constant supply of drugs to help with the pain. The three of us spent ten hours a day at Dad's bedside. We'd have done twenty-four hours a day if we could. We wanted to make the most of every precious second with Dad. He even found it in himself to be cracking his usual jokes to the nurses, he had them in hysterics some days. Typical Dad, making light of it all. He was doing his best to make it easier for us. We saw his pain, he wasn't fooling us.

Every now and again, his mask slipped down to reveal the vulnerable, dying man that he was. He wasn't afraid to die, he was afraid of leaving us. Our protector was leaving us behind. Those hours and days at the hospital were hard on us all, but the worst was yet to come.

THE HOSPITAL SPA

Five days became five weeks. The operation was probably the worst decision that Dad had made. His quality of life was declining fast. Mum, Hayley and I were reliant on the kindness of family and friends to transport us to the hospital on a daily basis. Every day, we would go to be with Dad, and his face lit up when we came around the corner. I asked if I could sleep over with him, but that was not permitted. Ten hours minimum, each day was spent at his bedside.

We had to make sure we were there for Dad when he needed us the most. He clung to us so much that leaving at the end of each visit was difficult. He would wave us off until we were out of sight. The crying on the journey home was the hardest part of each day. Would Dad make it through the night? Would his departure from this world be when we were not there holding him? That thought each day was torturous for us all.

The complications after the surgery were devastating. Dad suffered a lot, and every day, we dealt with a different problem. He was unstable most days. His blood pressure was dangerously low, and the alarm on the monitor would go off regularly. The nurses would run in to assist him. My heart was breaking more each day. He could not stand the pain and not even the morphine could bring his pain levels down to a bearable level. I wished I could take that pain from him. This proud man was losing his dignity in ways that I never imagined possible. He had a catheter that needed to be changed regularly to accommodate the large blood clots that he was losing. He cried for it to be removed. "I just can't take this anymore, I just want to die," he would say. We all hugged each other and cried together. That was the start of my wishing his life would end. I hate to think about that now, but those thoughts came regularly throughout the weeks that followed. It was just not fair to see this amount of suffering. He did not deserve this at all. He convinced the medical team to remove the catheter tube and this gave him immense relief from the pain that it had caused. He cried so much—we all cried together. He just wanted it to be over with. We all did.

We had made a family decision that we had to stay strong for Dad. We decided that pampering him and having that close contact would help him a lot to cope with the situation he was in. He was the envy of every other patient in the ward! We set up a daily spa for him. Hayley was doing his feet for him. Trimming his toenails, washing his legs and slathering on the cream afterwards. She was welcome to that job. There were limits to what I could do and feet were a no-go area for me. We did laugh every day about that. Dad would joke that Hayley was an expert in that field, and she actually turned out to be pretty good. My job was to do Dad's hands. I would soak his fingers in a bowl to clean his nails, then file them neatly for him. He was always a meticulous man and lying there in that hospital bed with no strength to shower or move around was an ordeal for him. We had to give him at least some of his dignity back. Dad also loved to have his hair combed and each day, Mum or I would be on hair-brushing duty. He loved it. His eyes were hollow, but they did gleam whilst we were there taking care of him. The nurses would be in awe of the attention that we gave to Dad. There was nothing we could do to take away the pain, but the least we could do was show him how much we loved him the same way he loved us all. I never really realised just how deeply he did, but our daily talks and outpourings at that hospital made it quite clear how much his family meant to him. He was a man of few words where emotions were concerned, but we learned how deep his love for his family was. We were his everything, the centre of his universe, as he was ours.

Each lunchtime, we would go for lunch at the hospital canteen. We ate because we had to and hated leaving Dad, even just for that short time. On one particular day, it was mentioned that a physiotherapist had to get Dad out of bed and mobile. We were horrified! How the hell was he going to gather the strength to walk? They brought the frame to the bedside, and Dad ushered us all away to have our lunch. We did not want to go, but looking back, I realised that he did not want us to see him struggle. He was frail and very weak, so this was going to be very hard for him. We gave him the dignity he desperately needed, and off we went for lunch. I cried all the way to the canteen. I did not want to leave him. We ate our lunch together in silence and took more time than we usually did, giving dad the necessary time he needed to have his first physio. We got back to the ward, and Dad's curtains were pulled around the bed. My heart was beating out of my chest, scared of what I was about to encounter. We all went, and there was Dad sitting on a bedside chair, shaking uncontrollably. He was in so much pain, and he was losing fluids from everywhere. Scared stiff and unable to move, crying whilst waiting for our return. Why did we leave him? I battle with that even now. Why did they make him get out of bed and walk?! I was furious. I ran off to find the nurses to come and help and voiced my feelings about the events that led to this situation. The nurses came to the rescue and got Dad topped up with pain medication. They stripped him down, changed his clothes and got him back into his bed. He never wanted to do the walk, and in the days prior, he was told he would need to be out of bed and moving about. Why? He was dying. What was walking going to achieve? It was never mentioned again after that day.

One nurse in particular, my namesake Tracey, was an absolute angel. She really took Dad under her wing and on her shifts during our weeks there, she would bring us coffee so that we did not have to leave Dad's bedside. One particular day, she got Dad on his feet and was more or less waltzing with him by his bedside. It was so beautiful to see, she felt like part of our family and was there at Dad's beck and call, plumping his pillows or just joking with him made a whole world of difference. We were and still are so grateful to her for all of her care and empathy.

Dad's surgeon often came to say hi to us all. He had explained that he operated on Dad like he was his own father. He was so obviously devastated that his attempt to extend Dad's life was not successful. He did everything he could, the risks were all discussed beforehand and Dad chose to go through all of this, albeit regretting it all.

Billy was a Chinese doctor who regularly checked in on my dad. He became quite attached to us as a family. He was a very kind young man who baked us brownies and delivered them in person to Dad's bedside most days. We just could not believe that we were all treated with such kindness. A doctor doing long shifts and then finding the time to go home to bake for us. Dad was not able to eat them as his appetite was practically non-existent, eating barely enough to keep a bird alive. We, however, looked forward to his delicious offerings. Dad was a VIP guest on the ward. It warmed our hearts to see how respected he was by so many people in the hospital. Not just staff but residents, too. It was a great help to us all during the many hours we spent there.

The spa days continued daily, making Dad as clean and as comfortable as we could. As the days passed, he was able to do less and less. Surrounding him with our love was the only thing we could really do. There was not a moment when Dad's hand was not held by his bedside. Breathing in the wonder of him. Why would we have wanted to be anywhere else? Nothing else mattered to us. Imagining a future without him was painful. Unbearable pain from the grief of losing him. The grieving process had started from the day we were told his condition was terminal. Losing a little bit more of him each day was crushing me to the point I could not breathe. The constant running to the corridor to let out the tears that I had struggled to keep inside, being consoled by the nursing team. Wherever he was going, I wanted to go with him.

We talked to him for hours about our memories... going back to the past helped a lot and Dad just loved that we could talk about that together, and it meant a lot to him that we remembered it all. He loved his life when we were all little, and the holidays and adventures we had were special. Sitting at his side in the hospital one day, I took him back to the days of our camping holidays. I could tell he wished he could relive all of that. Mum, Hayley and I laugh about those memories. His eyes glazed over. He could see our gratitude for the life that he had given us.

THE GREEN BUG

Dad was scurrying around packing up our shiny, green Morris Minor. The same routine every year, cramming everything into the car in preparation for our annual two-week holiday to Cornwall. How the hell did he get everything in that car? God only knows! First to be placed was the huge orange tent and awning on the roof, tied down with ropes and bungee straps. Once firmly placed, it was covered with the ground sheet. A camp kitchen, pots, pans, food, sleeping bags and clothing were crammed inside every single nook and cranny. The seats and footwells were piled high! Seatbelts were not compulsory in those days, and it was just as well because there was no way we would have been able to put them on.

The embarrassment whilst that car was

being loaded was something I'll never forget. Hiding away, watching everything being extracted from our huge shed and being literally stuffed into that miniature car. Never mind how he got everything in that car... how would we all fit in? The last to be loaded was Mum, me, my two sisters and our Sausage Dog Cassie, literally crammed in like sardines! We lived in a cul-de-sac and whilst we were the lucky ones getting a holiday every year, the thought of the many kids in our street seeing this minute car being piled high was really more than I could bear.

Once we were ready to set off, it seemed that every kid in the street was there to wave us off. "Come on, Dad, let's get going."

Dad put the key in, and then it happened: the dreaded splutter. That only meant one thing: the crank handle. Dad got out of the car to crank-start our little green bug. After several attempts to crank the engine, the car eventually spluttered to life. It isn't that easy to shimmy down out of sight when you're sitting on so much stuff, and your head's practically out of the roof... I wished I was invisible.

Now, in the 70s, the roads were not what they are now and that journey from Plymouth to the farm campsite in the deepest depths of Cornwall seemed to take an eternity. All squashed in with barely room to breathe, not that breathing was that easy with all the windows up and Mum and Dad chain-smoking the whole way! There I was, throwing up in my beach bucket whilst complaining that my sisters were touching me or breathing the wrong way. How they survived that journey with the stench of my vomit and Mum and Dad's fags was something short of a miracle. After what seemed like hours of torture and several games of eye spy (in between my vomiting), bobbing along the familiar winding country lanes, we were nearing the campsite. Our first port of call was the supply shop. We were all extracted from the car one by one, and we went to the shop. It was like an Aladdin's Cave and it sold literally everything! The Calor gas bottle was purchased along with our holiday treat of sweets and a new colouring book with felt tip pens. We were all carefully shoehorned back into the car to continue the last leg of our journey. Just a few miles more and we would reach our holiday camp that became a familiar part of our childhood.

THE FARM

Unloading the car was done with as much military precision as loading it. We were all ushered out of the way so that Dad, with Mum's help, could erect our huge, orange tent. Once the tent was up, the awning was attached. This housed the camp kitchen, pots and pans and all sorts of paraphernalia. Two weeks' worth of tinned food and a sack of spuds were all stacked in a corner. It was amazing the meals mum created using tinned steak and baked beans. Not all our meals were cooked in our tent. Lunches were a treat and mainly consisted of Cornish pasties or fish and chips. We would eat our fish and chips out of newspaper on a seafront wall with a wooden fork. Mum, Dad, me and my two sisters all tucked into our gourmet lunch, well we thought it was anyway, whilst Cassie the Sausage Dog was patiently waiting for a few scraps of our lunch. He went with us everywhere and was an important member of our family.

Halgarrack farm was tucked away at the end of a bumpy lane with no tarmac. We loved going there every year. It wasn't a fancy campsite, but we had the warmest of welcomes. Jim was a stocky man who always wore a flat cap and braces and Mary was a tiny lady with bright red lipstick. Her lips were very thin so she used to paint on the lipstick to make them look twice the size. Mary used to feed dozens of feral cats, so every evening, we were summoned to help her. Stale bread, warm milk, cat food and any other leftovers were put in a huge bowl and mixed together.

"Come on, come on, come on," she used to shout in a high-pitched voice. We all had to say it with her and sure enough, one by one, the army of cats came to eat their dinner. Jim used to take us on tractor rides around the farm's many fields. We'd be in the trailer loaded with hay being bounced around for what seemed like hours. It was so much fun. We would go every evening to the farmhouse for a fresh orange. They had them delivered by the sackful, the sweetest, juiciest oranges we'd ever had.

I now realise that our time spent being entertained by Jim and Mary gave Mum and Dad a well-earned break from us all. Mum and Dad were like pigs in the proverbial, sitting in their deckchairs outside their tent, which was their pride and joy, having a tipple or three. The St Michael's Mount Inn was a gorgeous, traditional country pub and was located at the end of the lane from the campsite. Some days, on the way back to the farm after a busy day exploring, we'd call in for refreshments. Mum and Dad were in the bar and Cassie, me and my sisters were in the family room. There was a rather convenient serving hatch, which meant Mum and Dad could pass through bottles of pop with a straw and packets of crisps. We absolutely loved it, but there was only so much pop you could drink.

"Come on, it must be time to go now!?" We would all leave there to go back to the farm. Dad drove up the bumpy, pot-holed lane with his leg hanging out the door, making us laugh, he really was so much fun. I'd give anything to be transported back there now, all of us together having the best time. When you're a kid, you don't really know how lucky you are. I know it now, I really do, and I'm so glad to have had my childhood. The sacrifices my mum and dad made so that we could have such wonderful holidays every year is something I'll be forever grateful for.

Dad's job was not an easy one and those weeks spent in his beloved Cornwall were a real escape for him. We went everywhere in that little green car. We scoured every country lane. Dad knew those roads like the back of his hand. We visited old tin mines, theme parks, the model village, a seal sanctuary and many other exciting places. Every year, we would go to a country show with steam engines and vintage cars. Dad's eyes used to light up! Steam rollers, lister engines and all sorts of vintage vehicles all lined up, looking shiny and new. I didn't have the same appreciation as a kid, but I can see now why dad would have loved it all so much. Dad went to a garage every year to get a huge lorry inner tube. We'd pack up the little green bug with our buckets, spades, and the huge, inflated inner tube tied to the roof. We had so much fun in the sea, and we were the envy of the other children, having this huge inflatable that was big enough for our family of five! One of my funniest memories was of Dad sitting in his deckchair reading his paper the whole day, wearing a string vest! We all laughed so hard when he took off his vest and was covered in red and white squares. "You look like a tea bag, Dad." Dad was not impressed.

Please, somebody invent a time machine. I want to go back to the good old days when we were a family of five, a whole family. My memories are keeping my precious dad alive right here with me. He had a plan all along.

SENT HOME TO DIE

The weeks at the hospital seemed like months. Each day was very long; we were all tired and drained, and at every obstacle, we thought Dad was leaving us. He was literally fighting for his life, not wanting to let go. Enduring enormous amounts of pain and suffering. His pain and suffering were also ours. I was willing him to let go, not able to utter those words to him, but willing God to take him to a better place. He was eating and drinking less and less as each day passed. He would ask Mum to bring him a certain food from home, and he would literally take small bites then give it to us to put in the bin. I struggled to cope with that, and on occasion, my emotions got the better of me. "You have to eat it, Dad. You need your strength," I would say. I realise now that his body did not need to be nourished. It was at the point where the digestive system was closing down. He got thinner and thinner as the days passed by. We stopped pressuring him to eat. This was such a hard thing for us all. Watching him literally waste away before us.

The palliative care team and stoma nurses stopped by each day to monitor Dad's condition. They were preparing us all for Dad's discharge from the hospital. A plan was discussed with us. Nurses would visit us at home twice daily to help with Dad's general needs. The nurses would be at our disposal once Dad's condition worsened... *How could it get any worse than it already was? Could we cope?* I was so scared and wondered where I would gain my strength from. God only knows I needed all the strength I could muster for the final stage of Dad's life. I felt weak, but Dad needed to see me strong. Everything I did in my life was to make him proud, and this was no exception. I had to be strong, not just for him but for my mum and sister, too. We all needed each other.

A hospital bed was ordered and was to be delivered to our family home along with other essential things that Dad would require. The day came for the delivery and Hayley and I stayed at home to rearrange the lounge furniture to make space for the bed. We waited at home for the delivery, and a more painful reality set in. The bed was placed. The bed that Dad was going to die in and in the home that had been ours for fifty-four years. More tears flowed. How could this be happening to us? Why?

We took photos of the lounge to show Dad. He had given us instructions on here he would like his bed placed. We booked our taxi to the hospital to spend the rest of the day with Dad. We showed him the photos that we had taken, not only of the bed but the whole house and his treasured garden. He was so looking forward to getting out of the hospital and could not wait to be back at home. He was very thankful to us for everything. We were thankful for him. Every day he stayed with us was a blessing. As painful as it all was, it was still a blessing.

That evening, we hugged Dad and promised to be there the following morning early. Mum, Hayley and I spent that first evening in the lounge having to look at that bed. It was so heartbreaking. We got through that evening and went to get some sleep. Sleep did not come easy to any of us but we needed to rest as much as possible.

The following morning, Mum's phone rang at a very early hour. It was the hospital... had Dad passed away whilst we were sleeping? Mum answered her phone in a panic. The nurse explained that Dad was in a complete state. He had been moved to a private room during the night as his bed on the ward was needed by another patient. He had woken up in a panic and thought he was in a mental home, in a room that was flooded with water. It, of course, wasn't flooded. He had lost control of his bodily functions and was very delirious. The nurse gave the phone to Dad, he was begging to speak to Hayley. She tried her best to calm him down. He thought they were going to hurt him. He was reassured that everything was okay, that he was safe and that we would be there very soon. We called a taxi to take us to Dad. He was a pitiful sight when we arrived. Scared and imagining he was seeing all sorts of things. The delirium had set in and was something we had been told would happen towards the end of life. "It's okay, Dad, we are here now," we said. It was time to fast-track him home.

The stoma nurse came that day to see us, and she told us that one of us needed to learn to take care of Dad's stoma. Hayley chose to do that and was trained very quickly in readiness for Dad being discharged back home. Dad also had a fistula in his stomach and that needed to be taken care of, too. All we had to do was wait for Dad's medication to be prescribed, and then an ambulance was to be booked to transport us all home. The drugs were dispensed along with a "Just In Case" box of medication. This was only to be administered by a registered nurse. The drugs we all dreaded. The drugs that would be needed at the very end of life.

Hayley and I packed up all of Dad's belongings, including the teddy bears we had bought to keep him company during the hours that we had to leave him. We were all ready to get out of the hospital and the support network was all in place ready for us. Being at home was where we all needed to be. It was Dad's wish to die there. The ambulance was called to transport Mum and Dad home and Hayley and I got a taxi booked so that we could be there to welcome them home. The nurses who cared for Dad during those five weeks, the surgeon and doctors all came into Dad's room to hug him and say goodbye. It was overwhelming, to say the least. All were lining up to say goodbye to someone they had only recently met. He had made an impact on their lives, he had a habit of doing that. I felt at that moment so proud of him. I always had a reason to be so proud of him.

My sister and I were back at home, making sure everything was in place for Dad to be as comfortable as possible. Finally, the ambulance pulled up outside. Dad was home. Home where he belonged. He was carried up the steps and into the house and placed in his reclining chair in front of the TV. The remote control was already there waiting for him. The ambulance crew left, and we were there, just the four of us, all just so relieved to be back home again. The colour in Dad's cheeks appeared. Mum made him a cup of tea, and there he sat in his chair in charge once again of the TV remote.

We all chuckled about that. It was nice to have that moment of normality. It felt like home.

Our family home and we were so happy to be there together again. He sat there for hours watching his favourite TV shows and old movies. I just could not stop looking at him, taking in all the wonderful things that I had to be so grateful for. The things I took for granted suddenly meant so much to me. At the end of the afternoon, it was time to get Dad into bed. He had a frame that he had to use to get about, not that he could get about that much. With the aid of his walking frame and me and my sister on each arm, we gently guided him to his bed and got him all snuggled in for the evening. There he lay, falling in and out of sleep, looking so happy to be back in his familiar surroundings.

I did not want him to be left alone, so I suggested that I sleep in the lounge with him. He needed twenty-four hours of care and supervision and I could not leave him. Mum and Hayley agreed as long as I went to wake them if there was any problem. Off they went upstairs to bed and I got comfortable on the sofa next to Dad. The first night of the many nights that were to follow. Each night was spent mostly watching him, making the most of him whilst I still had him.

AROUND THE WORLD ON YOUTUBE

Now, Dad was not one for traveling, and I am pretty sure that he would never have vacationed in Spain if I had not moved there. The same went for his visits to Australia to see his brother and sister and their families. He was a simple man who loved his creature comforts and was more than happy to do his local day trips around Devon and Cornwall. He was passionate about where he came from and would speak for hours about where he was born, places he went etc. I was always captivated by his stories about his childhood and his adventures with his father, my grandfather. He literally had me in stitches whilst he relived his memories. He was a good storyteller, but invariably, he could not finish speaking because he laughed so hard. "What is so funny, Dad?" I used to say.

"I know what's coming," he'd say, so the stories were never fully finished because he was in hysterics. His face used to balloon and turn bright red, tears rolling down his face whilst he rubbed his eyes. Those memories are etched clearly in my mind. He was hilarious. His ability to make people laugh was simply amazing. He was known for a lot of things and being a funeral director was only one of them! His jokes were not always the best, but how he had memorized so many was just incredible.

My adult life was always filled with traveling, and Dad used to love following my adventures on YouTube. He traveled everywhere with me from the comfort of his armchair. He was so proud of me, I always knew that. In every country that I visited, Dad wanted to visit with me virtually. Every trip I made back home, dad would want to know all the details, and we would sit together doing a virtual walking tour around the places I had been. I loved that he was so interested in my adventures.

On one of my visits home before his diagnosis, we were talking about my travels. "If there was anywhere in the world you could visit, where would it be?" I asked him.

"Portofino," he replied. That prompted him to put Andrea Bocelli in concert in Portofino on YouTube. He was mesmerized by it. We sat watching the concert whilst Dad's eyes shone. My head was buzzing with ideas. I was going to arrange that trip for him for his eightieth birthday. The surprise trip was arranged but did not happen. Dad never got to visit Portofino.

Our YouTube tours each day became an escape for us all whilst we were nursing Dad. A way of taking our minds away on adventures, escaping the sad reality that suffocated us daily. Virtual coastal walks around Cornwall. We visited all of our favourite seaside towns that we had seen so many times in reality whilst we were a young family. Dad could literally imagine us all there eating our Cornish pasties or our fish and chips on the beach. Priceless, beautiful memories that helped us all to cope. One of the tours we did many times over those weeks was around Gretna Green, where Mum and Dad had eloped as young adults to get married. We saw the townhall, the villages around and even were shown the car that they had eloped in! It was like watching a movie! Surreal circumstances and there they were, so many years later, sat watching this and holding hands. Mum didn't want Dad to leave her, but staying as strong as an ox for us all, she kept it all together. Tears rolled down my cheeks as I watched them both with glassy eyes, reliving their most memorable adventure that had taken place fifty-nine years before. How proud I was to witness such a beautiful moment. Another precious moment and memory made at the saddest time of our lives.

My dad was renowned for visiting the garden centres. How many times have I been dragged along to a garden centre? There are too many times to count! But he loved to walk around for hours telling us the names of all the shrubs and flowers, educating us on plant life. What we looked forward to the most was the cream tea in the café at the end of it! The day after, we did it all again, albeit to a different garden centre and a different tearoom. We had to think of ways to transport Dad back to relive his favourite pastimes, so on some days whilst we were caring for him, we would find as many things as possible for him to watch either from his bed or his armchair.

One day, Mum and Hayley were upstairs cleaning, and I was sitting with Dad. "I have an idea, Dad, let's go to the garden centre," he looked at me with a puzzled look on his face whilst I took control of the TV remote and scrolled to find a walking tour. Lo and behold, I found some. *Oh, how he loved that!* He could not believe that someone had actually been to do a walking tour at his favourite garden centres. We sat laughing our heads off. I shouted up to my mum and sister, "Hurry up, you two, we are going on a trip." Then they came to the lounge to find me and Dad waiting to go on yet another virtual trip. They were laughing hysterically at my idea and Dad sat patiently waiting for the tour to begin. There we were, sitting comfortably, drinking cups of tea and doing the once dreaded walks around so many garden centres, but in the comfort of our living room. Dad was dozing in and out of sleep whilst we laughed as a family. He loved to hear us laughing, moments like these I will always cherish. We were making memories but did not realise it at the time. I just sat there wishing with all of my heart that we could jump in Dad's car and go off for the day. In reality, we knew that was never going to happen. Sitting there that afternoon and seeing Dad's face light up was just amazing. We all had to be creative about keeping Dad's spirits up, and this was not an easy task. Inside, we were all finding our strength dwindling. It was becoming harder and harder to find the energy to cope, but through it all, Dad kept us going. He was our tower of strength even when he was dying. We were supposed to be his.

One evening, around a week after Dad had been sent home from the hospital, we talked a lot about his friends from his working days. He just absolutely loved to talk about that. He took a lot of pride in his profession and was looked up to by so many, even years after he took his early retirement at the age of fifty-five. We talked about his colleagues who had become part of our family over many years. He started telling us who he wanted to be present at his funeral. It was such a shock to hear him talking so openly about the guest list for his funeral. "I want Peter Morgan to do my funeral, Sue," he said.

"We have to invite him over to have a chat about it." I just could not believe what I was hearing. I stole myself away yet again to hide from everyone. Locked away in the bathroom sobbing my heart out, the pain was incredible. He was still with us and there he was talking about his funeral. The first time of many times in the days that followed.

THE VICAR CAME TO TEA

Mum was busy in the kitchen the whole morning. "What are you doing, Mum? You've been in here for hours!"

She swiveled around to face me, looking flustered and completely covered in flour! "I've got to make an effort. Father Morgan is coming to tea!" She had more flour on her face, in her hair and on her apron than was in the food. There was definitely a resemblance to Casper the Ghost, she looked more like she had been preparing herself for a Halloween party! We did have a few hours before our guest was arriving, but looking at the state of the kitchen, we would need a divine miracle to clean it all up in time. I did laugh, but I know that mum was pleased to have the distraction and something else to think about, other than the reality we were all faced with.

Mum took pride in her baking and was known to produce delicious pies and cakes. She just knew that her offerings would go down a treat with the Vicar, a portly man who clearly loved his food. The delicious smell was wafting through the house. Three batches of pies were made, in and out of the oven, one batch at a time and then neatly arranged on plates, along with the cakes and covered, ready to be presented to our honoured guest.

The cleanup operation began in earnest, and my sister and I tackled it at great speed. We washed all the baking tins, cleared the worktops and hoovered up the snow-like covering that was all over the floor. "All done, Mum," we said, and with an hour to spare.

Whilst we were all busy in the kitchen, Dad was in the lounge making his own preparations for our important visitor. Father Morgan and Dad went back a long way and did many funerals together over many years, including several of our very close family members. The impending funeral was not just anybody's funeral, it was my dad's. This discussion we were about to be part of was not one that I looked forward to.

Dad was sitting in his chair with his little grey notebook. Jotting down notes and instructions for his final departure. He beckoned us over to read his notes. There, in his book, were his wishes and requests:

- HYMN – Dear Lord and Father of Mankind.

- PRAYER – The Lord's Prayer.

- CURTAINS – To Remain Open at the End of My Service.

- SCATTERING OF ASHES – Under the Memorial Tree at the Cemetery.

It was so hard seeing his notes there before us. Staring us in the face was a more impending reality, the inevitable reality that we did not want to think about. "Are you happy with what I have chosen?"

After a few moments of silence, I responded, "I think you are definitely the expert in these matters, Dad and I just know that what you have chosen is going to be perfect for you." Mum and my sister agreed wholeheartedly with my reply. It was hard to know what to say because it's not every day that you are faced with discussions like these. Dad had spent the best part of his life arranging funerals for other people and now was faced with arranging his own. We knew that him making his own arrangements was a deliberate act on his part. He was preparing us for what was to come, trying to soften the blow and ease the pain for us. A selfless, lovely man. I will always be so grateful to him.

Dad patiently sat there armed with his notes that were held tightly in his hand. I, on the other hand, excused myself for some private moments. Locked away in the bathroom, tears flowed— silent, gut-wrenching tears that just didn't want to stop. The bathroom became my hiding place many times throughout each day. The place where I could be alone, locked away so that my grief and pain were hidden from my darling dad and from my family, who were struggling to cope with their own sorrow. The tears came often and crept up on me day and night. I felt suffocated with grief, it was as if a big black, Grim Reaper-like cloak was being draped around me as I cried those painful tears. Guilty tears, too, because Dad needed me to be strong. How could I be strong? I was losing the man I loved and looked up to the most in the world. I gave myself a good, hard-talking, too. I had to pull myself together...

Father Morgan arrived on time. Mum scurried to the door to let him in. "Come in, Peter." Dad beckoned him from his chair. *What was happening?* I thought to myself, *Dad is not posh*. Dad's voice was suddenly all very well-spoken, which made me chuckle inwardly. A rare moment to smile, which I was grateful for. Dad was Cornish and definitely didn't have a posh accent, not even a posh Cornish one. The mood had definitely been lightened, another of Dad's tricks to calm our nerves.

We all sat there in the lounge, chatting for what seemed like hours. Dad and Peter reminisced about days of old. Chatting about mutual friendships and all manner of things. For a moment, Dad was not sick anymore, he was our old dad laughing and remembering old times. Good times when he was doing the job he loved. He was a true gent and a highly respected pillar of the community. Everybody loved him, and I am quite sure He will always be remembered by all who knew him.

Mum went to the kitchen to fetch the pies and cakes and placed them on the table in front of Peter. "My gosh, Susan, you have done a splendid job," he said. Peters' posh, loud, bellowing voice held court during the whole afternoon. I suppose this was beneficial to him whilst doing his sermons at the church. We all sat lined up like his congregation. He knew us as children and was very keen to know how our lives had been shaped. Imagine this jolly, posh-speaking Plymothian Vicar in our lounge, giving all of his time and my dad loving every moment of it.

Peter had retired some years before, so we were all very honoured that he would come out of retirement, especially for our dad. Sitting there that day listening to him, it was evident why my dad wanted him to take care of his last farewell. This special, kind man thought the world of my dad, and we will always be thankful to him.

Dad's little grey book was still in his hand. No mention of its contents was uttered. That afternoon was a real gift for my dad. A few hours talking about his precious family, about the job he loved, was all the medicine he needed that afternoon. The book was put back in the drawer for another day.

Peter had devoured several meat patties and some cake, all washed down with a cup of tea. It was time for him to go. It was clear that Dad was very tired from all the trying to be normal and not sick. He was absolutely exhausted. We all bid Peter farewell, and he promised to visit again soon.

Dad was helped from his chair to his bed in the lounge. My sister and I held him whilst he shuffled along to his bed. We made him as comfortable as we could, and there he slept for hours whilst all we could do was sit and watch him, not wanting to miss one second of the precious life that was slowly leaving us all behind.

THE LAST VISIT TO THE GARDEN

The hospice nurses continued to come in during the day to check on Dad. He would hold court, telling them his stories whilst trying to mask the pain he was really feeling. They would ask him how he was coping with things and his response was the same every day.

"I am okay, I have everything I need right here. My family is looking after me well." He just wanted us to know how much he appreciated everything. The care he got at home was all he needed, making the most of us as we were him. Our daily spa treatments continued. As his pain worsened, we pampered him more. Brushing his hair, holding his hands whilst he felt our unwavering love and we felt his. The closeness we all felt whilst we were caring for him was a real coping mechanism. He always held my hand with a firm grip, rubbing his thumb in the hollow between my thumb and forefinger. I still feel it now. I grip my own hand often in the way that he did, I feel like he is still here with me, holding my hand. I am quite sure that he is.

We laughed at the jokes that he had saved for the carers' visits, but the jokes became fewer and fewer as the days passed by. The jokes that once were mocked and cringed at were becoming something I pined for. I hear them in my mind even now, but the scary thing is they are fading gradually from my memory, which terrifies me.

Dad spent the days either in bed or in his reclining chair and could shuffle about the house with his walking frame whilst we all walked with him, holding him up. On one particular sunny day, we suggested that we help him to the conservatory. It took some time to get him there, but once we did, it was worth the effort. We sat him in his chair, which faced out into the garden. The garden that he had spent many years transforming. It was brimming with colour. The gorgeous shrubs and trees were there in all their glory, waiting for Dad to visit. He struggled to get warm even though the sun was shining.

Mum sat in the chair next to him, holding his hand as I watched from behind. They sat there just savoring the moments together, looking out at the garden and watching the resident birds flying in and out of their bird boxes. A tear slid down my face as I watched them. Silently, I watched them and just wondered how on earth Mum was going to live the rest of her life without Dad. Her life partner was leaving her. I secretly took a photo of them both as they sat there, and I crept away, leaving them to each other. That memory is etched firmly in my mind and literally tugs at my heartstrings.

Hayley and I joined them an hour or so later in the conservatory, and we all sat there drinking tea, admiring the garden. Dad was so proud of it and had spent many hours over many years looking after it. It was his pride and joy. That day was lovely, it gave us all a few hours of distraction, something we all needed at that time. We escorted Dad back to the lounge, washed and dressed him in his night clothes and got him settled for the evening. We called the nurses to say that Dad did not want a visit that evening. He wanted to just lay there in his bed. We talked a bit more, reflecting on the lovely afternoon spent in the conservatory. More wonderful memories were made and stored for our new future.

The next morning, the hospice nurses came in to see Dad. He seemed brighter on this particular day. They gave him a wash and dressed him and had their usual chats with him about his life. Some people really are angels without wings because those nurses cared for Dad so well, the empathy and love that poured out of them was just amazing. The same amount of love and empathy was also given to us. They were as much there to support us on our difficult journey of losing our precious dad as they were there to care for him. Shortly after the nurses had left, Dad called us. Off we went to the lounge and there was Dad up on his feet, holding his frame. "We are all going to the garden," he said. I looked at Hayley, she read my mind. *How the hell were we going to get Dad up into the garden? He could barely walk in the house, and getting to the garden involved uneven paving stones and steps.* We told Dad that we would do our best, but it was not going to be easy. We got him to the conservatory and sat him there in his chair. This was the halfway mark of the journey, and he was tired already.

"Just sit there for five minutes, Dad, we are going to the garden to prepare your seat there," I said. Off we went to the garden and voiced our concerns to each other. *How were we going to get him there?* It was not going to be easy, but we knew how important it was to Dad, so we agreed we would get him there.

Dad was gripping his frame, and Hayley and I held each of his arms to steady him. Mum was walking in front to guide him. He shakily stepped over the conservatory threshold and into the first part of the garden. We strategically placed his frame on each step up to the garden. Two steps up, then we shuffled along the crazy paved path. We slowly made headway and arrived at three more steps that were barely big enough to accommodate Dad's walking frame. We held onto him for dear life and we did it! There we were on the patio. We were all shaken up. We sat him in his chair and covered him in fleece blankets. The sun was out in all its glory and flooding the patio with warmth. Dad sat there all wrapped up, his frail body swamped in blankets, basking in the sunshine. Mum sat beside him, and Hayley and I excused ourselves to go in and make some tea. We went inside, and both cried. The fear that had built up getting Dad into the garden was just awful. "We got him there, sis," I said. We both knew at that point that was not the hardest part. Getting him back down again was going to take some effort. *How were we going to do that?*

We carried a tray of tea up to the garden and sat for a few hours chatting together whilst Dad slept. He looked so fragile sitting there. We tried to forget that it would soon be time to get Dad back inside the house, but we knew we had to hatch a plan. Dad woke up. He was completely drained and had to be taken back inside. There was nothing else for it, we braced ourselves and got to work. We uncovered Dad and got him onto his feet. We sensed that he was as afraid as we were. He stood there gripping the frame, ready to make his journey back to the house. The first three steps down took quite some time, he was shaking. Dad was frail and had lost a lot of weight, but it was still hard for us to hold him up. I had tears building up inside me. I could not lose it at that moment, I had to be strong, literally. We got him back onto the path, and he did his best to shuffle along. He was tired and lost his strength. "We won't let you fall, Dad, not far to go now," I said. It might not have been far, but it felt like a mammoth journey. We got to the top of the last two steps and Dad started realizing that he just might fall. Panic gripped him. He took one hand off the frame and grabbed the garden hedges. He was falling, and we had to muster up all our strength to save him. "Hold the frame, Dad, we've got you." It took some time to get him down the steps and onto the small patio at the conservatory doors. Mum grabbed a chair, and we sat him there to steady his nerves. When he felt ready, we got him into the conservatory and slowly made our way to the lounge. We carefully placed him in his armchair to recover. He was exhausted physically and emotionally—we all were.

I went up to the bathroom, locked the door and stayed there until I had stemmed the flow of my tears. The shock and realization that our once strong dad was now reduced to this fragile wreck. Did we regret the risk we took getting outside for the day? No, we did not. He never asked for a lot, and just seeing him sitting there in the sunshine in one of his most treasured places was worth all the risk. Our dad had a lovely day. It was to be the last time he visited his garden. His garden will miss him. The resident birds will miss him.

THE EMERGENCY CALL-OUT

Dad was sitting in his recliner with the sun streaming in through the bay window. He loved to sit there watching the neighbours going about their business and seeing the children playing in the street. The same street that I played in as a child. The view of the river and the boats was something that kept him living in that same house for so many years. All of my memories, as far back as I can remember, involve that street and those views. I sat watching him, wondering what was going through his mind. He had no idea how long he would be able to see those views, to see the leaves blowing in the tree that had stood tall for so many years at the entrance to our house. He knew he would not see it for much longer. The simple things in life that he cared about the most. He was definitely not a materialistic person, and his priorities were definitely in order.

Hayley came into the lounge and broke the silence. She was coming in to check on Dad's stoma and fistula. She lifted Dad's clothing and reeled in shock. Dad's fistula was losing blood, it was pumping out of his stomach like a volcano erupting! I ran over to help her. We literally had to peel off the fistula cover to replace it with another as it was overflowing, pressing down on the opening to try to stop the flow. Mum ran in to see what was happening. "Call an ambulance, Mum," Hayley said. Mum went off to call 999 and insisted that an ambulance come as soon as possible.

Dad sat there bewildered, but instead of panicking, he was trying to calm us. "It's okay," he said. "Nothing to worry about..." *Nothing to worry about?! He was losing so much blood and all I could think was that we were losing him there and then. Was he haemorrhaging?*

71

Hayley was crying, it was all too much for her. She had been responsible for a lot of dad's care but this was just more than she could handle. "I can't do this anymore, Dad," she said. Tears were running down her face and just feeling so bad that she had reached a point where she could not cope anymore. "Dad, you need proper care, more care than we can give you here at home," she said. This was to be the start of a dreaded conversation about managing Dad's symptoms in the Hospice. I did not want this. Dad wanted to die at home, surrounded by his family and in familiar surroundings.

The ambulance crew arrived and took over from us. We stepped back and gave them the space needed to work on Dad. We stood there watching helplessly. They managed to stem the bleeding for a while, checked his blood pressure and prepared him for a trip to the emergency department. Now, I know Dad was craving a day out, but that was not the day out we had in mind.

The ambulance crew allowed us all to travel to the hospital with Dad, and upon our arrival, they kept us in a holding bay outside. Shortly after, a team of medics and a very nice doctor came to assist Dad in the back of the ambulance. It was explained that it was safer to treat him there as he was at high risk of infection if he had gone into the building. We were there for around two hours and after many tests, they were happy for him to be taken home. The bleeding had stopped. Thank God. Once we had been delivered safely back to the house, Dad was carefully carried up the steps to the front door and was taken inside. We got him washed and changed, ready for bed and made him comfortable. We were all on autopilot, our nerves were shot to pieces. Mum and Hayley went up to bed and I got settled on the sofa next to Dad, holding his hand and chatting about the day's events. Our chats each evening, whilst it was just the two of us, were very intense. We would talk until exhaustion took over, and he'd fallen into a deep sleep. I, like every other night, lay there watching him. Watching his breathing patterns, literally terrified that he would leave us whilst we were sleeping.

The following morning, the Hospice nurses arrived to wash and dress him. After an hour or so of hearing them chatting and laughing, we stole them away to have a private chat. We explained the situation to them, and we all came to the same conclusion: he needed more care than could be given at home. We all needed respite from the situation, so we agreed to broach the subject to see if Dad would agree to a stay in the Hospice. We all cried, and the nurses hugged us and explained that it was for the best. We needed to have some rest from the situation if we were to be strong enough for when things were to inevitably get worse.

We returned to the lounge and sat with him and explained that it was just all too much to deal with at home and that he would get better care and supervision if he agreed to it. Dad sat there smiling and nodding. "It's a good idea," he said. He knew St Lukes well because he had been on many occasions to remove residents who had sadly passed away there. He and his hearse were regular visitors there over the many years that spanned his career. Little did he know then that he would be faced with staying there himself. He explained that he knew about the care and love that they gave to everyone who came through the doors. There he was, yet again making it easy for us. He did not want us to go through any of it, even more than he wanted to go through it himself. The decision was made and arrangements were put in place for Dad to be transported there that same afternoon.

Mum made a pot of tea, and we all sat with Dad, reassuring him and loving him a whole lot more for his strength. His strength gave us strength. If he could stay strong whilst enduring what he was going through, then so could we. We laughed and talked about things in general, but inside, I was crumbling yet again. Dad was going to the hospice, not because he wanted to. He was doing it for us. How would I live with allowing that if he had taken his last breath there and not in his home?

Mum's phone rang. It was the Hospice to say that the ambulance was on its way to collect Dad. Hayley and I stayed behind to pack some clothes and toiletries for his stay. We watched him being carried down the steps whilst Mum followed behind. She looked worn out and defeated as she followed Dad into the ambulance. The doors were shut, and off they went on their journey. I cried. Hayley cried. Was this to be the last time dad saw his home?

ST LUKES

Hayley and I arrived at St Lukes in a taxi. We both took a deep breath before going in through the doors and painting smiles on our faces. We were met at the reception by a friendly lady who led us into Dad's private room. There he was, propped up in a bed which faced the huge windows. The building was in a stunning location with views over the river and was surrounded by gardens. This was fabulous for him, and we could see that he was happy enough to be there. Dad was pleased to see us back with him. He hated us being separated, and we wondered how we would cope leaving him there in the hospice each night. We had a chat with the head nurse, who encouraged us all to stay with dad. We were totally amazed that we could all stay in the room for the whole of his stay! Hayley and I called a taxi to return home to pack a bag for us all. Dad's face literally lit up. It was obvious that he was having the same worry about us leaving him. "Lovely," he said. He was over the moon that we could all be together and continue the difficult journey together as a family. "Don't be long. Hurry back," he said, and off we went to our waiting taxi.

A short while later, my sister and I returned to the hospice with essentials for us all for at least a few days. We had no idea how long we would be staying. We put our clothes in the wardrobe and placed chairs around Dad's bed. It was a relief to be together once again. We placed all our Spa equipment on the locker beside the bed and set about our usual routine of pampering him. I brushed his hair whilst Hayley cleaned his feet. Mum sat there holding his hand whilst they chatted away animatedly. It was an absolute vision, and another memory was made.

The nurses came in to introduce themselves

and Dad was smiling from one ear to the other and getting lots of wonderful attention. It wasn't home, but it didn't feel like a hospital either. These carefully trained nurses were there to give their support and to make our dad as welcome and as comfortable as possible. Bedding was placed on the sofa and the chairs for us so that Dad could sleep surrounded by his family.

The hospice had a huge spa bath which had hoists to help the patients in and out. Dad had not had the luxury of a bath or shower for many weeks, so we spoke to the nurse and asked if they could bathe Dad. We mentioned the bath to him and he was nervous at first because he was so weak, but he was quickly assured that they would help him and he would be absolutely fine. I was overwhelmed that this simple pleasure was now something my dad would appreciate so much. The nurses helped Dad out of bed and placed him in a wheelchair. Mum followed Dad off to the bathroom whilst my sister and I sat in the room and waited for their return.

We heard him coming down the corridor before we could even see him. He was back to his usual chirpy self making the nurses laugh. He came into his room looking shiny and new. Literally sparkling clean! The colour had returned to his cheeks, and suddenly, he looked loads better. Dad was helped back into bed, and we all sat there hugging, holding hands whilst Dad joked about the fancy spa bath he had just had. The lady from the canteen came in with a menu. "Choose whatever you want for tomorrow's meals, Leslie," she said. It was like staying in a hotel! Dad had not eaten much at all for a few weeks, so we were shocked when he ordered a full English breakfast and a roast lamb dinner. No way was he going to be able to eat all of that! We stared at him in amazement and thought that the stay in the hospice was not going to be so bad after all. He had a new proverbial spring in his step, and it was so lovely to see. Hayley and I excused ourselves to give Mum and Dad some time alone, and we went to make a cup of tea in the canteen. We were told to help ourselves whatever we wanted and to make ourselves at home. We made the tea and took it to a beautiful summer lounge which overlooked one of the gardens.

"Let's take Dad out tomorrow to the gardens," I said, knowing that he would love that and the fresh air would be good for him. Hayley agreed that the following day, after breakfast, we would take him out. We sat there chatting for an hour and returned to our parents. Dad was now very tired from the day's events, it was time to settle him down for the night. I got comfortable on the recliner next to Dad's bed, and Mum and Hayley got onto the sofa bed. We dimmed the lights, and all said good night. None of us really slept, not just because it wasn't comfortable but because it was such a worry that Dad could die in the hospice. That was something that none of us wanted. Least of all, Dad.

The following morning, we all got washed and dressed and were ready to have our breakfast. The breakfast trolley was wheeled into the room and Dad sat up in bed whilst the food was placed before him. The food on that plate was more than he had eaten in the previous two weeks! Mum had her breakfast with him, and Hayley and I went to the on-site cafe to have ours. We sat eating our breakfast chuckling, wondering how much of the breakfast would be eaten. We were just so happy that he looked brighter and did seem to be better. That was sadly not to last for long.

We ate our breakfast and went back in to join them. Dad had miraculously eaten half of the food. We just could not believe it. The nurse came in to remove his tray, and as she was leaving, he called out, "I could murder a nice cup of tea!" *What happened to the man we brought in the day before? He was a different person in the space of one day!* She reappeared a short while later with a tray of tea for us all, and we sat there together, just enjoying each other's company.

"We are going on an adventure, Dad," Hayley said. He looked confused but excited by that prospect. Hayley disappeared and came back a short while later with a wheelchair and two nurses in tow to help him out of bed. Dad was dressed and wrapped up in blankets, and in no time at all, he was ready for his adventure. We took him on a tour of the hospice to show him all the lovely lounge areas and the cafe and then proceeded to take him outside. Of course, he already knew that hospice well, but he really appreciated the effort we had made for him. He looked so vulnerable and fragile being wheeled around, but he really did love it. We showed him all the gardens, a fishpond with huge coy carp and then up to the most special part of the gardens. It was accessed via a snaking path to a flat viewing platform, and there before us was the most incredible view of the river and the surrounding countryside. He could not speak for a while as he was overcome with emotions. Hayley was in control of his wheelchair whilst Mum walked beside them. I was behind, taking it all in whilst taking photos on my mobile phone of the wonderful moments that were unfolding. More moments for our memory bank. It was getting cold so we all went back into the warmth of the hospice. The nurses appeared again to help Dad into bed so he could get cozy and warm again. The food trolley appeared with dinner, but it was turned away. He was too exhausted to face that. The day went by in a flash, and before we knew it, it was time to retire for our second night there.

Dad's condition over the following days deteriorated. His ambitious attempt at eating his meals soon wore off. His body did not need food anymore. The baths he was offered were refused, as were the meals. He had a few visits from precious family members, but he hardly had the energy to communicate. Conversations became more difficult as his pain worsened, and he told us many times he just wanted to die, it was his time. By the eighth day, as a family, we decided it was time to take our Dad home. We spoke to the hospice team, who agreed that it was time to go, and the home care team was put in place to resume their visits to our house. Dad was delighted to be going home, he missed it so much. We just knew that our time together was drawing to a close. We gathered our belongings and waited for news that the ambulance was on its way to transport us back to the place where he wanted to die. He wanted to die at home, surrounded by the family he loved, in the privacy of his own home.

DISAPPEARING ACTS

We were all just so grateful to be back home in familiar surroundings. Dad quickly settled back into the routine of the "Angel Nurses" visiting at home, and our love and care were magnified. My calls to my husband became few and far between, his need to be with us was great, but I selfishly needed to keep him away. I did not need the distraction and wanted to be with Dad, giving him one hundred percent of my attention. I would need Rob in the very near future but not at that moment.

My evenings with Dad in the lounge after Mum and Hayley had gone to bed were spent talking as much as possible about everything that Dad thought was important. We reminisced about the days gone by when I would help him proofread his obituaries. Every night after school, once my homework was finished, I would sit with Dad whilst he did his paperwork. I loved that he included me. I was the eldest and always was a bit of a bookworm, so I was delighted to help him. We talked about the hearses he would bring home from work on his lunch breaks. You can imagine what my friends thought about seeing Dad's hearse parked up outside our home on a regular basis! Why was he talking about the hearse? Was this yet more preparation for the impending events that were due to happen at any time? Dad went quiet, and his mind wandered off...

"Did you see the will yet," he said. I did not want to talk about his will. He was still with me, it was too painful to even think about.

"Yes, I have seen it. It's okay, Dad," I replied.

"What about that Just In Case box of drugs we were given?" he looked at me with an imploring look on his face.

"It's okay, Dad, that's safely stored away in the dining room," I said.

"What exactly is in it?" he asked. I knew where that conversation was going. He wanted me to discuss in detail what all the drugs were and what they would be used for. I went to the dining room to get the paperwork that was sitting on top of the locked 'Just In Case' box and only accessible to the end-of-life care team. I sat next to him and went through the list with him. One of the drugs was for agitation and sickness, and one was for delirium. I explained that at the end of life, it was possible that he needed sedation to calm him and to make his exit from this world more peaceful. The conversation was not an easy one, and explaining it all in detail was difficult to do when trying to choke back my tears. Dad sat nodding, absorbing all the information I was giving him. "Make sure I am sedated," he said. He repeated himself several times, and I agreed that if, in the event, it was deemed necessary, we would make sure he got a sedation. "Get me my little grey notebook," he asked. I went to retrieve his book from the drawer and took it back to him. He opened the page to his funeral wishes and started reiterating his wishes for his funeral. I sat as best I could, listening avidly to him. That book was last opened on the day that Father Morgan came for tea and there it stayed in that drawer untouched until that moment. He was talking in depth about his memorial tree. The tree that I was actually taken to many times, even before Dad's diagnosis. He wanted me to know even back then that he was going to be scattered under that tree. He talked about all manner of things relating to his funeral. I sat there whilst silent tears slid down my face. Just Dad and I were in the confines of that lounge, talking about his death and his funeral. Dad noticed my tears and held my hand.

"It's time for me to go, Tracey. I have had

enough now!"

The tears were flowing in torrents at that point. I gripped his hand tight and said, "I know it's time soon, Dad and just so you know, if I had to choose my dad. I would choose you one hundred times over." We cried together, and I fell asleep, holding his hand through the safety bars on the side of his bed.

I woke up with a start in the early hours to check on him. He was gone! Where the hell was he? In a panic, I threw off my blanket and went to the kitchen. Dad was gripping his walking frame and standing by the back door in the kitchen. He had gotten there with just his frame but could not get back. My heart was racing because I was scared about what I might find. "I am okay," he said. I told him he must not do that again because I felt responsible for him and that if he had an accident, I would have blamed myself. "Keep this between just you and I," he said as I helped him back to his bed in the lounge. I told him that if he needed anything, and I was asleep, he must wake me. I have a hearing impairment and couldn't hear clearly. I refused to sleep for the rest of the night, in fear that he would hurt himself whilst I was sleeping. The little Teddy Bear that I gifted him whilst he was in hospital was placed on the bed beside him. "If you need me, Dad, and I don't hear you, throw Teddy at me."

He rubbed his eyes whilst laughing his head off. "Great idea," he said. Teddy was thrown at me on a regular basis from that moment on.

The following morning, I took my mum and sister to one side to explain about the night before. I did not want to break Dad's confidence, but it was important that they were aware of the situation in case something did happen. The care team came to see Dad and monitored his condition. The pain was on the increase, so it was decided that he would need to have his medication dosage increased. Whilst the nurses were there, we gave dad some water. As soon as he swallowed, he started choking. The nurses proceeded to tell us that now was the time to stop all liquids and solids. Not that he had consumed much in the days prior to that. We were faced with literally watching him starve. Drinking the fluids was now a danger to him as they were going straight to his lungs. "Can I give him Ice Poles?" I asked. They told me that, yes, he could suck on some ice to soothe his mouth, which was becoming very sore. How could we deny him water? My heart broke a little bit more.

The day quickly came to an end. Mum and Hayley hugged Dad good night and I settled next to Dad. We chatted for a while, and then I dimmed the lights so that we could get some rest. I was just dosing off to sleep when I was hit by the Teddy! I looked over at Dad and there he was, chuckling. He still kept his sense of humour even in the last days of his life. We laughed and both drifted off to sleep.

During the night, I sensed something was wrong and woke up with a start. I had strategically placed myself next to the bed so he could not get out. The other side of the bed was positioned against a bookcase and fireplace, so I did not think he could get out of bed on that side. "Oh my God! What are you doing, Dad?" There was Dad stuck at the side of his bed, holding the mantle piece and squashed into the tiniest of spaces. I leaped off the sofa and onto his bed to go to his rescue.

At that exact moment, Mum burst into the lounge. "What the hell is happening?" she said. There I was, standing on top of Dad's bed and Dad gripping onto the fireplace. He had escaped again! Mum had to squeeze herself into the small space to help me maneuver Dad back into his bed. We got him back in, and I had to run. I just could not stop laughing. It was like something from a comedy sketch. I laughed so hard all the way to the bathroom and literally wet myself leaking. I locked the bathroom door, sat on the loo and the laughing turned into heaving sobs. The laughing happened a lot. It was not funny at all, but I now know it was the shock of everything I was dealing with. I was living an absolute nightmare of which I had no control.

THE ONE BLUE GLOVE

Mum, Hayley and I sat in the conservatory eating our breakfast in silence whilst the nurses were tending to Dad. It was becoming more and more difficult for us all. We all knew that we would be saying goodbye to him soon. Father's Day and my birthday were looming. No day was a good day to lose him, but I prayed that it would not happen on either of those days. Those days needed to be memorable for the right reasons. The nurses came for a chat with us when they had finished helping Dad. They commented on how much he had deteriorated. Every day, he was fading more. He had lost his spark, there were no more jokes to tell. I spoke to the nurses. I needed to know how long they thought he had left. I literally wanted him to die. Thinking like that was killing me inside, but seeing him suffer was just too much. We were all struggling with the thought that he would soon be gone, but we could not bear to see him suffer. They told me that, in their opinion, it would be quite soon. Sadness washed over me, I was drowning in grief. They sat us down and explained that we were at the stage where we would benefit from having a night nurse. I sat and cried. I did not want a stranger in our family home. I wanted it just to be us, our close family. Mum and Hayley calmed me down. "Let's give it a try," Mum said. Reluctantly, I agreed to it, but as long as I could stay with my dad during the night. The nurses went on their way, and we sat with Dad. He was sleeping most of the time, so we just sat chatting together, taking turns holding Dad's hand or brushing his hair. We wanted him to feel cloaked in love. He was not leaving this world alone, and we made damn sure about that. My aunt and uncle came to visit and Dad just lay there. He had lost the will and energy to speak. They loved him so much, and this was going to be just as hard for them. They were an enormous support to us during this whole ordeal and we could call on them at any hour to help. They stayed for an hour, then hugged us all goodbye. We waved them off, and there we were again, just the four of us together. The afternoon went by quickly, the days seemed to get shorter and shorter. Time was running out.

The doorbell rang. I slowly went to the door to reluctantly greet the night nurse. On the doorstep was a lady dressed all in black clothing, wearing a black hat and carrying a black rucksack. She smiled at me as I let her in. I explained to her that I would spend the night in the lounge next to my dad and that she was there only to observe and help if necessary. It soon became very clear that this was a big mistake. Mum and Hayley went off to bed and I promised them that I would fetch them straight away if they were needed. I made myself comfortable next to my dad and held his hand. He didn't stir, he just lay there. The night nurse made herself comfortable. She was barely visible as it was so dark, and she was dressed from head to toe in black clothing. I did not feel at all comfortable with this arrangement. The private moments I wanted with my dad were taken from me. I lay there for a while listening once again to Dad's irregular, laboured breathing and drifted off to sleep.

Dad suddenly threw off his bed covers. The agitation had gotten worse over the previous few days, but this evening, it was bad. I woke up and went to calm and comfort him, his arms reaching up as though he was seeing something. *Was he seeing something or someone?* The nurse got up and put on a blue rubber glove... Not two gloves, but one blue rubber glove. She approached Dad's bed and tried to calm him down. Her manner was not great, and I am quite sure that she had no clue what she was doing! Dad was asleep when she arrived, and this was the first time he had set eyes on her. Towering over him, looking more like she was about to go on a bank heist! I asked her politely to sit on the sofa and observe from a distance. She made her retreat and left me to deal with it. As a family, we had managed for many weeks, and at this last hurdle, I did not want any interference. I eventually managed to get Dad settled and calm and thought it was time to get my mum and sister.

I went up the stairs as fast as I could and gently woke them. Bleary-eyed, they got out of bed. "I think it's nearly time," I said. We all made our way back to the lounge to face the long night ahead. The three of us surrounded Dad's bed to comfort him. His agitation grew worse throughout the night, and calming him became more difficult. Every time that Dad had an episode, the night nurse would come up to the bed waving at Dad with her one blue glove. *Did she think it was a glove puppet? That dad was a child?* My patience was wearing very thin. Dad was very delirious and had no clue what was going on, which was just as well because I am very sure he would have sent her on her way. I could not take any more of this ridiculous behaviour.

Dad was sleeping again, so I took the opportunity to deal with the nurse. "Can I have a private word, please?" I asked. She followed me out of the lounge into the kitchen. "Please don't take offense, but we need you to leave," I explained in a very polite manner that she was adding no value by being with us and that we had realised that we wanted to be with Dad in privacy as it was clear he could be taking his last breath at any moment. She looked rather bewildered but said she respected our wishes. She went back to the lounge to retrieve her belongings, and I let her out of the front door. I took a deep breath and composed myself before entering the lounge.

"Where has she gone?" Hayley said.

"She's gone. We don't need her here," I replied.

Mum joined our conversation, "Thank God for that. What the hell was she doing wearing a beanie hat and one blue glove!"

My hysterical laughing started again, and I ran like the clappers upstairs to the bathroom, wetting myself on the way. Once again, my hysterical laughing became sobbing tears. I hated myself for laughing. There was nothing to laugh about. I cleaned myself up and made my way back to my family. The three of us surrounded Dad and stayed there the whole night. We did not sleep. We spent the whole night doing what had to be done together as a family in the privacy of our family home. Dad's episodes were hard to cope with, but we stayed strong for him.

Tracey Van Der Veer

JUST IN CASE

Dad was nearing the end of his life. We reached a point where we dared not leave his side. His breathing was becoming more and more laboured and noisy. *The Death Rattle,* they call it. The weeks that led us to this point could not have prepared us for what we were faced with on this day. His delirium and agitation had reached a point where we could not calm him. Together we discussed the Just In Case medications and came to the conclusion that now might be the time to think about that.

Dad was awake on and off throughout the day. The nurses came to tend to his needs and were also of the opinion that Dad's body was in the final stages of closing down. He had a driver for the drugs wired into his leg whilst he was in the hospice, and now they were explaining that it was time to use the end-of-life medications. I went to the dining room to fetch the box containing the medication. I felt numb, it was hard to breathe. *Would Dad even know we were with him?* I had to hope so. The drugs were necessary so that Dad would be sedated in a peaceful state. At least we would not see him suffering anymore, so there would be at least one consolation. Mum, Hayley and I made our way to the conservatory and left the nurses with Dad. We all sat there together, crying and holding each other. The end was coming. It was hard to imagine a life without him.

One of the nurses came to find us and explained that they had increased the medication in Dad's driver. They would have to be topped up and administered gradually over the coming days, and his condition would be monitored. If at any time his condition worsened, they would return to us immediately. They hugged us all and gathered their things, leaving us to have our precious dad to ourselves.

Dad was calmer than in previous days, thanks to the drugs they had given him. He did wake up a few times and constantly told us he loved us all. He was literally fighting now for his life, but he needed to let go. We gave him tiny crushed pieces of ice to soothe his mouth, which was now very sore. We brushed his hair, stroked his face and not even for one moment was his hand not held. He was leaving this world cloaked in our love for him.

Suddenly, Dad reached out to Mum and hallucinated that Mum was offering him a glass of water. He was trying to grab the glass that was not there. Hayley and I hugged and calmed him whilst he was literally begging for the water. Mum had to leave the room crying. She had stayed so strong up until that point.

Once Dad was calm, we went to find Mum. "How can I not give him water?" she asked. We held her, and we all cried. We had to deprive him of even the simplest of things like water.

We explained to Mum that he would drown if we gave it to him. The water would go to his lungs. After a few moments, we all composed ourselves and made our way back to Dad.

His episodes of agitation were getting worse, so we called the nursing team, who then made their way back to us. Dad's driver was adjusted so that the drugs would be fed into him faster, and once again, they hugged us all. They felt our pain, they had also grown to love my dad. It was so hard on them, too. We knew how much this was affecting them. We waved them off, and once again, we were all alone, the four of us.

It was time to tell Rob and my darling children that the time was nearing. Rob had been on two occasions whilst Dad was in hospital after having his first operation, as did my children. Dad even met his two newest grandchildren while he was in the hospital, which he absolutely loved. He made it clear afterwards that he did not want them to see him so ill and that he wanted them all to remember him as he was. I locked myself away in the privacy of my bedroom and made painful video calls to my children to tell them. I said that they must not come but to remember their grandad as the kind, funny man that he was. The memories they had of him were priceless. One memory they often spoke about was their grandad playing basketball with them. I say play basketball, but he was just fooling around. They were told they had to call him Lou Lou The Dribbler, which used to make them howl with laughter. I reminded them of that memory during the call that I made. We cried together. They loved their grandad so much, and all his many grandchildren did. My sister's children did visit, too, before Dad got too poorly, but they were also kept away after. That was Dad's wish, which, of course, we honoured. He was right!

It was then time to call Rob. It was the call he was dreading but had been waiting for. He did not want me to go through this without him. I had his support during the whole journey. He allowed me to be with my family without any complaints and he knew and respected that I was needed more by my family, which I will always be grateful for. If it was possible to love him any more than I did, my love for him grew more.

I called Rob on a video call and I didn't even need to speak. He knew that I needed him. I updated him as best as I could through the tears. I needed him more than I ever needed him. "Please book your flights and come as fast as you can," I said. He rushed me off the phone so that he could book his flights. A short while after, Rob called back to say the earliest flight he could get was for the following morning, and we prayed that he would make it here on time. Hayley had made her call to Mark, and he immediately got in his car to make the three-hour car journey to join us. We had both decided to be away from our families and were both blessed to have such loving, understanding husbands who put our needs before their own. Soon, they would be with us to support us and to say their own goodbyes to their father-in-law. They loved and respected him like we did. They were the sons that he never had.

I returned to the lounge to hold my dad's hand. There we all were, watching his life slowly slip away. We all felt it would be very soon. We spent the rest of the day doing everything we could, knowing it was not enough. Nothing could change the situation. We could not keep him with us, as much as we wanted to. His suffering had to end, as did the suffering that we were enduring.

Mum made her way up to bed and Hayley and I stayed in the lounge together for a while. "Put Andrea Bocelli on YouTube, sis," I said. She took the remote and found Dad's favourite video of his concert in Portofino. There were the beautiful sounds of his voice singing *Time To Say Goodbye.* Hayley cried silent tears listening to that. We hugged goodnight, and I lay next to my dad, listening to the soothing music. I hoped that he could hear it. It really was time to say goodbye. I lay there holding his hand through the bars of his bed and watched him the whole night.

LET GO DAD

Mum and Hayley could not sleep and came to join Dad and I in the early hours of the morning. We all sat there together, knowing the clock was ticking fast now. Mark arrived to join us, so I went to the kitchen to make some tea. We sat there quietly, and the silence was only broken when Dad had become agitated. His agitation seemed to worsen even more that morning. Reaching skyward a lot, it was as if someone was beckoning him. I got comfort from thinking that his heavenly family was waiting for him, calling him to them. It was time to call the nurses again to increase his medications.

We opened the door and let in the nurses. Once again, we fetched the locked box of Just In Case drugs and left them alone with Dad. "It's time to call Father Morgan," Mum said. We agreed that it was indeed time so off she went to call him. He promised to be with us as soon as possible. The next call was to our aunt and uncle; they had been a huge support to us all and we know that Dad would have wanted them there with us. Mum called them to tell them it was time to come to say goodbye.

My aunt and uncle arrived and were followed closely behind by Father Morgan. "We will leave you to have some quiet time with Dad, Father Morgan," I said. He told me it was not necessary and that he wanted us all to be together. He opened the bag that he had brought and robed himself. He was there to read Dad's last rights. *How sad but painfully wonderful was that?* It was as if my dad was holding on for this to happen. We all surrounded Dad's bed whilst Father Morgan anointed Dad with oils, making a sign of the cross. He prayed for him and read the Lord's Prayer:

*Our Father who art in heaven, hallowed be thy
name.*

Thy kingdom come.

Thy will be done

*on earth as it is in heaven. Give us this day our
daily bread, and forgive us our trespasses,*

*as we forgive those who trespass against us, and
lead us not into temptation,*

but deliver us from evil.

*For thine is the kingdom and the power, and the
glory, forever and ever.*

Amen.

We all said *Amen* through sobbing cries. *How
did it come to this?* Father Morgan hugged us all,
and we thanked him for his presence and the
friendship he gave to my dad over so many years.
He removed his robes and went to say goodbye
to Dad. Just as he approached him, my dad
reached out for him. A beautiful moment was

witnessed and will stay etched in my memory forever.

The front door opened and in walked Rob. He had made it! I was so scared that he would not arrive in time. Another person that Dad had waited for. I hugged him so hard and cried so much. I had not wanted to keep him away, but now he was here, and I needed him. I sent him to see my dad, he had missed the visit from the vicar, but he had made it in time to say his own goodbyes. He went to see Dad and spoke to him. Dad was not awake, but he knew he was there. He knew we were all there. His precious family meant more to him than anything else in the world.

The nurses had to be called again. Dad suddenly took a huge turn for the worse, and we could not control his agitation. They quickly arrived, and we had the box of drugs there waiting. There was no time to lose. The drugs were administered very quickly, and although it helped with the agitation, his breathing was terrible. I have never heard a noise like it. It sounded like he was suffering; we were assured—he was not—I struggled to hold in my sobs as I watched on helplessly. We all held each other tight. The nurse made a call to the hospice to get her permission to administer the final drug. The permission was granted, and the medication was administered. We were told that the drug would help as it was the maximum dosage, and once again, we were left as a family unit together.

We were all so worried that Dad might be suffering because the noises he was making were getting worse. His body seemed to be convulsing. "Please let go, Dad," I said through heaving sobs.

"Let go, please." I gripped his hand tightly. Mum and Hayley gripped the other. We all, one by one, gave him our permission to leave us whilst we held and stroked him, and, there in the comfort of his own home, surrounded by his loved ones, he took his last breath. We all comforted each other. Mum clung to Dad, crying. Her life partner had left her. She had stayed strong for him—we all did. Now, we had to be strong for her. She hugged him for a while, then went over to the windows and opened them wide. "Let his spirit out," she said. I covered Dad's body, leaving his face exposed and closed his eyelids. We called the nurses again to say that Dad had passed away. They returned quickly with a doctor who checked all of his vitals and confirmed that he had passed.

We all sat together in the lounge, crying, chatting and talking about good things. That is what Dad would have wanted. The pain of his suffering left my body, the grief never did and never will. An hour went by, and it was time to call the Undertakers. The same company that Dad had worked for, for so many years. Whilst waiting for them to arrive, I lay on the edge of the bed, hugging my dad whilst everyone chatted around us. I did not want him to be taken away, but I knew his spirit had gone on. This shell lying beside me was no longer my dad. My dad had gone to a better place. A place where he would wait and watch over us all until we could join him again.

The doorbell rang. It was The Undertakers. They had arrived in a van to collect my dad. How times had changed from the years before when my dad was working. He used to collect loved ones' bodies in a shiny hearse, not a van. *Where was the respect in a van?* My dad was always a stickler for tradition and I had imagined the tradition would be the same for him. I was devastated and even more so seeing them carry in the gurney to remove my dad from our home. He was carefully placed in a bag, which was then zipped up and placed on the gurney. We watched in tears as he was carried down the steps and placed in that van. It was the last time we would see him in our family home. We watched as Dad was driven away, and we all went inside to the eerie silence. There was the hospital bed, the blankets, the Just In Case box and all of the painful reminders that Dad was so ill. The cancer had beaten him, but he fought it all the way. My brave, wonderful dad gave it everything he had until he could fight no more. His suffering had ended.

Cancer does not define him. Many things define him. He was a good son, husband, father, grandfather, great-grandfather, brother, uncle and friend. FUCK CANCER!

THE LITTLE GREY NOTEBOOK

I felt numb. My new normal had just begun and it was a normal that I never wanted. A life without my dad was hard to imagine and was something I had always feared. The days before my Dad's departure were spent, willing him to die, to free him from suffering and pain. Now he had gone I selfishly wanted him back. I would never get to hug him or hold his hand, to hear his jokes. Our family puzzle was incomplete.

Rob sat hugging me in the lounge whilst I stared at the empty hospital bed. My face was wet from the constant flow of tears. I had cried for weeks, but these were different tears. The pain felt from this huge loss was something that I was not prepared for. I felt empty and lost. How was I going to move on? Hayley had Mark to comfort her, but Mum had lost Dad. How was she going to cope without him? She needed us more than ever now and we had to make sure we stayed strong for her. My mum's strength through it all had been incredible, but now we could all see that she was now broken. Dad had taken care of everything for her, so it was time to take her under our wing and help her move on to a new life without the man who had always meant the world to her.

That awful day came to an end, and we all went to bed. I had been deprived of sleep for so many weeks, but that night, I slept like a baby. The following morning, I got showered and dressed and made my way downstairs. I stood still at the entrance to the lounge and, after a few moments, opened the door and went in. The hospital bed was still there, we were told it would be collected in a few days... a few days! How could we cope with looking at that? That bed represented suffering and pain, and none of us wanted to look at it. My eyes swept around the room, and I settled on the empty reclining chair—the chair was my dad's. The TV remote control was sitting on the table beside it. He loved to take charge of that remote control, taking us all down memory lane. All I had now was the beautiful memories that he created for me. It suddenly dawned on me that he could make no more. I was alone in that room, just trying to take in the scene before my eyes, the tears flowed again. I stood in the bay window looking at the tree at the foot of the steps, its leaves were blowing in the wind. The view of the river and boats in the distance that Dad loved so much, a view that he would never see again. The neighbours were going about their business and the children were playing in the street. I made my retreat from the lounge and closed the door behind me. I could not bear to see any more of it at that moment. I made my way to the conservatory to join my family. Their faces were stained with tears, it was raw. We all felt lost and helpless but knew that we all had to stay strong. We all hugged and comforted each other and braced ourselves for the day ahead. The first day without our leader.

Mum made a pot of tea and we all sat together in the conservatory, looking out onto the beautiful garden that had evolved over so many years. The resident birds continued to fly in and out of their bird boxes. Did they know that my dad had now gone? I stared into the distance and my mind drifted off to my childhood days in that garden.

Dad pulled up in the funeral car outside our house after a long day at work. He was always dressed immaculately in a pin-striped suit, white shirt, black tie and highly polished shoes. I saw him walking up the steps and ran to greet him. It was a very sunny summer day. I can remember it clearly. "Come on, let's go to work in the garden," he said to us all. Dad had a push along lawn mower in those days, nothing as posh as an electric one. The garden was on a slope and was mostly lawn with shrubs around the borders. It was one hell of a lawn to mow! He took off his jacket and tie, changed his shoes, rolled up his shirt sleeves and off he went to the garden. We all followed along behind him, knowing that we had our work cut out for us. Dad walked up and down that garden for what seemed like hours! Pushing his mower through the long grass, making it all neat and tidy whilst we waited in the wings. Our job was to rake up the grass and put it into bin bags.

My sisters and I gathered all the grass cuttings and scooped them into the bags. "Get me the shears," Dad shouted. It was time for him to neaten the grass borders.

Off I went to get the shears and watched him working away in his garden. When it was all finished, he stood back to admire it. Plonked himself in a deckchair with a whiskey in his hand, ready to unwind from a long, hard day. No rest for my dad, he worked his fingers to the bone. His garden was the second most important thing in his life. His family was his first. My mind snapped back to reality, sitting there in the conservatory looking out into the garden, which was bursting with shrubs, flowers and trees, my eyes filling up with yet more tears.

We sat there chatting about memories, trying to focus on the positive things that we all had to be grateful for. We really did have a lot to be thankful for, but it was hard to appreciate any of it. Why did such a good man have to suffer? That was the only thing I could think about. Life felt so cruel at that moment. My amazing Dad, who spent his life doing for others, was taken away in the most awful way. Could I ever erase the suffering that I had to witness? I really don't think so.

I was dreading the discussion that was going to be necessary soon, albeit I knew it was necessary. It was time to talk about Dad's funeral. Off I went into the lounge to retrieve Dad's little grey notebook. The notebook had been stored away in the drawer of the table, next to his reclining chair. Its contents were not discussed when the Vicar came to tea. It was now the right time and arrangements were to be made. All of Dad's wishes were stored safely there inside that little book. I returned to my family with the book gripped in my hand. "Its time to call the Undertaker's Mum," I said. Mum took out her mobile phone and rang the number. She very calmly made an appointment for us all to visit them to discuss the arrangements for Dad's final departure.

APPOINTMENT WITH THE UNDERTAKER

A musty smell hit me as I entered the Funeral Director's building. The very same building that Dad had worked in for so many years. The floral carpets were the same, albeit now they were practically threadbare. The furnishings all seemed very familiar, too. We were all greeted by a lovely receptionist called Sophie. She knew my dad well. Even though he had retired many years before, he just could not let go and would often pop in to say hello to his ex-colleagues or to meet new staff. He was a regional manager for the best part of his career and was highly regarded in the profession. Sophie asked us to wait in the reception area and would call us when the private room had become available. Mum, Hayley and I sat there together, taking in the old-fashioned surroundings. There was a cabinet filled with urns and trinkets. We wondered if it was a good idea to have some of Dad's ashes made into jewellery. Dad would not have wanted that, we had been given clear instructions on what had to happen to his ashes. We felt he was with us. He never abandoned us when we needed him, and his presence was definitely felt that day.

My mind drifted off to the days when I would walk into town with Dad to buy Mum's Christmas presents. Being the eldest child, I was always taken with him to help choose her gifts. I used to love those trips with him. He would spoil Mum rotten with new clothes, shoes and perfume. On the way to the shopping centre, we would always call in to see Dad's work friends, and I would be in awe of him. The Big Boss was how I saw him. I always looked up to him. He was my role model and teacher. He helped shape my life and career. I owe so much to him.

Sophie called us into the private room, and we all walked in and sat around the dark wooden desk on old chairs. The same table and chairs that, no doubt, my dad has sat at so many times over the years. Today, he was with us in spirit. Sophie closed the door. I took a deep breath. Now was the time to discuss Dad's wishes. Mum pulled out the little grey notebook from her bag and proceeded to tell her that Dad had, in fact written down his wishes and also notes about the help that Mum would need. Mum also produced a funeral bond, which had been purchased many years before for them both. Everything had been paid for, including the coffin and the hearse. Before Dad passed away, he asked Mum to organize a special car for us to travel to the cemetery. Mum chose a beautiful Daimler which was going to transport us to say our farewell. He wanted to stick to tradition, and we wanted to give him the best send-off. He deserved that.

Sophie gave us some booklets with floral tribute ideas. We were to take them home with us and take our time over choosing the wreaths. We all talked openly about Dad's wishes, and it was noted that Father Morgan was to do his service. She knew Father Morgan well and was delighted to learn that Dad had chosen him. She made notes about the Obituary notice that was to appear in the local Herald newspaper. My mind went back to the days of helping Dad proofread the obituaries and now here I was helping to write his own.

"We need to prepare an Order of Service" Sophie said. We gave her the notes from Dad's little book. She made note of the hymns and prayers, and we were to send her anything else by email that we might want to include. We sat there for what seemed like hours but mostly talking about memories of Dad. Sophie said she had a list of Dad's work friends from the past and that she would contact them all to let them know he had passed away. There was no doubt that they would want to pay their respects to him.

Sophie promised us that they would take extra special care of Dad. He was in good hands and we knew it. We hugged her goodbye and she closed the door behind us. We stepped onto the pavement outside, a gust of fresh air blew through my hair and the musty smell of the Undertaker's office was no more. Mark and Rob had waited outside for us; they were there to hug and console us, and we really needed it. We made our way into the town centre and found a nice little coffee shop, and we went into the warmth. We sat there talking about Dad's funeral. We had all individually wished him free from suffering. We now wished it was all a bad dream. We wanted him with us more than anything now. We finished our coffee and it was time to head home.

We sat in the lounge, the hospital bed and

other paraphernalia still there, waiting to be collected by the hospital. I made a mental note to insist on it being taken as soon as possible. It was just too painful to see it all there. We discussed the contents of Dad's order of service. Mum chose some nice photos to include, and I asked if I could add a poem. I knew that I would not be able to speak at his funeral and I also knew that he would only have wanted Father Morgan to do the speaking. He was a stickler for tradition, and we had to see it through to the end, all according to his wishes.

"That's the picture that I want to go in the chapel with Dad," Mum said, pointing to a very beautiful, gilt-framed photo of Dad, which took pride of place on the living room wall. There he was, proudly sat behind the wheel of a vintage, open-topped wedding car, dressed in all his finery. He looked so proud with his cheeky grin and rosy cheeks. She chose well, it was the best photo of him and summed him up perfectly. "We have to take his clothes to the chapel of rest," Mum said. I felt blood drain from my face. Dad had actually chosen the clothes he wanted to wear to his funeral, and they had been hung and covered in his wardrobe for several weeks before his passing.

"I want to dress him," Hayley said. I just couldn't believe that she could be brave and strong enough to do that. Dad had actually dressed his parents and siblings for their funerals, and Hayley wanted to do this last honour for our dad. We all agreed that the next day, we would visit the chapel with his clothes. It was going to be another very difficult day.

The evening came and we all hugged each other goodnight. I did not sleep much that night. Did I want to see my dad in the chapel? Would he even look like my dad? I wasn't sure if I could cope with any more heartache. My grief pain threshold was being tested to its limits.

DRESSED FOR THE OCCASION

We all sat in the conservatory drinking tea whilst Mum was finishing getting herself ready. Suddenly, she appeared holding the covered clothes, all neatly arranged on a coat hanger. I was trying to push the pending events of the day out of my mind, but it was impossible. Mum proudly held onto Dad's clothes, she was ready. More ready than I was, and my poor sister Hayley had the hardest task of all. Dressing dad. I gripped hold of Teddy, he was needed to keep Dad warm.

We all got into Mark's car and off we went to the chapel of rest. We were all ushered into a waiting room which had modern furniture and a restful decor. Various staff popped in to see us to give us their condolences. They each had known my dad for several years. It gave us all peace of mind that Dad was indeed in very good hands. They were looking after him for us. A very nice lady came into the room to let Hayley know it was time to go and prepare Dad. Hayley looked white as a ghost as she clutched all of Dad's clothes in her hands. She followed the lady out of the room and shut the door behind her. The four of us sat there in silence, we did not know what to say. My only thoughts were of Hayley at that time. *How was she going to deal with seeing my dad, never mind dress him?* I watched the seconds tick by on the clock on the wall, the silence in the room was unnerving. My lips felt numb, my mouth was dry. It felt like we had been sitting there for an eternity.

The door opened, and in came Hayley. Her eyes were red and swollen. She was completely distraught. We all hugged her and told her how proud we were. And we really were proud of her. "I couldn't let anyone else dress, Dad," she said as the tears streamed down her face. My brave sister was in pieces. I now had to make the agonizing decision of whether I could cope with seeing my dad. I needed to see him. Rob held me and walked me and mum down the corridor to the room where Dad was waiting. I opened the door and quietly walked in. There was my darling dad laying on a metal table, dressed in his best suit, complete with shirt, tie and highly polished shoes. His hair was combed immaculately into place, his skin was shiny. He lay there with his eyes closed, completely still. Tears were burning my eyes, I went to him. I bent to kiss his forehead, he was so cold. He still looked like my dad. I had seen dead people before, and death had changed them. Not my dad, he still looked like my dad. He looked so peaceful and handsome laying there. A sudden peace came over me, a huge relief and realization that he was not in pain anymore. I held his cold hand, his fingers looked the same.

His nails looked neat from all of the spa sessions we had had. I caressed the hollow between his thumb and forefinger in the same way he had done to me. I carefully placed Teddy under Dad's arm. The Teddy that had brought us some joy whilst Dad was dying. I could not bear for him to be alone. Mum hugged Dad. Her life partner with the larger-than-life character was now laying there lifeless. No more jokes to be told. No more hugs. Thank God we had a lifetime of memories to bring comfort to us all. Mum's light had gone from her eyes. Her protector had left her behind.

Poking out of Dad's pocket was a furry hedgehog that Hayley had bought him, and then something caught my eye. Mum had placed photos of us all as a family of five. Photos of proud young parents with their three young children on a family holiday, with our Sausage dog Cassie. Rob walked over and straightened Dad's tie. He patted his hand and said a silent farewell to the man that he had respected so much. We made our retreat and shut the door behind us, leaving Dad in good hands. It was time to go home.

The hospital bed was collected later that day, along with all of the medical equipment. I was definitely glad to see that back of it. We all sat together that evening, talking about Dad. His reclining chair was still empty in the bay window. The TV remote control was perched on the table. Home was not home without Dad. Suddenly, it just felt empty and meaningless. He had made our house a home. I stood in the window silently, watching the boats on the river whilst the leaves blew in the branches of the tree at the bottom of our steps. I had to go home. I had been there for several months, and now I had to wrench myself away and go back home with Rob.

The following morning, at breakfast, I announced that it was time I left. Mum was relieved because she was also feeling the need to leave the house and it's painful reminders. I booked my flight to go home with Rob and Mum packed her bags to have a break with Hayley in Hampshire. We had two more painful weeks waiting until Dad's farewell, and for now, we all needed some detachment. Mark drove us to the airport, and Mum, Hayley and I hugged each other. We were each other's rock for so many weeks, and now we had to each find a way forward.

I arrived at my home in Spain. I dropped my bags and just sobbed. I had been away for so long. My home, my business and my husband had all been waiting for my return. It was time to move on but I did not know how. The two weeks that followed were difficult. We chose beautiful flowers for Dad's funeral. Hayley and I spelt the word DAD in beautiful yellow flowers. Mum had chosen a beautiful spray for the top of Dad's coffin, and my daughter Charlotte made the most beautiful floral display spelling GRANDAD in the most magnificent colours. All of the grandchildren contributed to the flowers and Charlotte was to make the wreathe. The Obituary was sent to me to read and an online editorial enabled friends and family to write their own tributes for my dad. It was heartwarming and humbling to see such a huge outpouring from so many people. Dad had meant so much to so many. The most painful day of my life was looming. It was time to book our flights back to the UK.

GOOD BYE DAD

1906 WOLSELEY

The tenth of July had come around quickly. The day we were flying back to the UK, the day before Dad's farewell. Rob held my hand tightly during the whole flight, he knew that I needed all of the support he could give. It was becoming more and more difficult to talk about things. The slightest thing made me cry. I didn't recognize myself anymore. I had aged considerably, the lines were now more deeply etched into my face. The lines showed my pain and sorrow. I never knew such pain existed. I do now.

We arrived at our family home and were greeted by Mum, Hayley and Mark. It felt like I had never been away. We had grown so much closer as a family during this awful time in our lives, and we needed each other now more than ever if we were to get through the next day. We all prepared our clothes for the funeral and neatly hung them up. Our shoes were cleaned, and everything was ready for Dad's farewell. We all wanted to look our best for him. My phone didn't stop pinging. Messages were pouring in from my friends, who had been a huge support. They were there when I needed them the most. Some friends did not even bother... they were obviously not real friends. My circle became smaller. My auntie flew in from Australia and other family members were making their way to Devon to bid farewell to an important man that I was lucky enough to call Dad. Father Morgan called Mum to go over the final details for the funeral. Mum, Hayley and I started preparing food and drinks for the wake. We were grateful to be so busy. The day came to an end and it was time to sleep. Sleep did not come. I lay there thinking about everything. Good and bad. I craved for Groundhog Day. I did not want the morning to come because that meant it was my dad's funeral.

We all got up and gathered in the conservatory. We drank tea, we could not face food. It was time to get ourselves ready, so we all, one by one, made our way to the bathroom to shower and dress. An hour or so later we all met up in the lounge looking highly polished, dressed head to toe in black. We were going to give Dad the best, traditional send-off, and we wanted to look our best for him. The hearse was due at any moment so we made our way outside of the front door to wait at the top of the steps. Time stood still. I am sure the boats were still bobbing on the river in the distance, and the leaves were still rustling in the tree at the bottom of the steps, but I didn't notice. My mind was blank, standing there waiting for my dad to arrive.

The highly polished, black hearse came around the corner and reversed up the hill. It came to a stop outside of our house. A wailing, guttural cry rose up from deep in my stomach. Dad had come home one last time, albeit in a coffin in the back of a hearse. We all made our way to the street and surrounded him. His coffin was draped in the beautiful flowers that Mum had chosen. The glass sides of the hearse displayed the flowers, DAD and GRANDAD. He loved his flowers and I know we did him proud with our choices. At the end of the coffin was the photo of Dad in the gilt frame. Standing there proud, looking out at us all. This was his last visit to our family home, it was time for his last goodbye to the fifty-four years of memories that were safely stored in the bricks and mortar of that house. We all got into the Daimler to follow him to his final destination. The neighbours lined the street to nod a farewell to Dad. The street will miss him.

We followed at a snail's pace behind Dad's coffin. We all sat in the back of the car, lost for words. The tears flowed abundantly. The car came out of our street and did a right turn into the street where our grandparents used to live. Both cars came to a stop outside my dad's parents' old home. A beautiful thing took place. He was also able to say goodbye to his childhood home. We had a minute or two in silence, then made the slow journey to the crematorium.

The hearse came to a stop about one hundred yards from the chapel, and the funeral director got out of the passenger seat and walked to the front of the car. Wearing a top hat and tails and carrying a cane, he bowed to my dad, turned and walked slowly to the chapel. Both cars followed behind him. There was a sea of people all there to pay their respects. Family, friends, work colleagues, neighbours and even some of the hospital and hospice staff who had taken such good care of Dad. There at the front of the chapel, I spotted Father Morgan, dressed in his Robes and gripping his bible. He was a good friend to Dad right until the end. He was honoured to be giving my dad his final farewell.

The tears kept falling, I was now faced head-on with the most difficult day of my life. I stood there surrounded by so many people being held and hugged by my beautiful children, who were as much there for me as they were for their grandad. Dad was carefully removed from the hearse and lifted by the pole bearers. They were made up of two of his brothers and ex-work colleagues. The colleagues who showed him the utmost respect when he was their boss and now showing the same respect in his death. We all followed Dad into the chapel and took our seats in the pews. On each seat was a beautiful order of service that contained the hymns, prayers and photos of Dad. On the back was the poem that I had asked to be included—a poem that spoke volumes about my dad.

We all sat there whilst Father Morgan led the service. His loud, bellowing voice filled the chapel. It was no ordinary service, it was also a personal tribute to a man that he held in high regard. A colleague and a good friend. He did my dad very proud and talked a lot about the man that he was. Dad was at the front of the chapel, draped in his beautiful flowers and his lovely face in the picture, looking out at us all. The hymns were sung, and prayers were said. Father Morgan's job was done. He pressed a button under his pulpit, and the curtains around Dad's coffin began to slowly close... "Stop, Father Morgan," I cried out. I went to the pulpit and explained that Dad wanted his curtains left open. He pressed the button to reopen the curtains and apologized. I know that Dad would have found that hilarious and maybe the joke was on him. We all made our way one by one to place a hand on his coffin and say our last goodbye.

Outside in the fresh air, I was surrounded by people who could not even fit in the chapel. I knew Dad was popular and I prayed that he would have a good send-off, but this was just incredible. I said thank you to as many people as I could, it was overwhelming. Close family members and friends made their way back to our family home to share a drink and some food with us. Hayley's best friend was already at the house and had travelled down from Hampshire with a carload of food, including cream teas. The food was all laid out ready, drinks were offered and Father Morgan took his seat at the head of the dining table and devoured the delicious offerings.

Everyone eventually left and then just the five of us sat there in silence, reflecting on the beautiful send-off we had given our dad. He would be so proud of us, we knew it.

When I am gone, do not fear my memory.

Do not be afraid to speak my name or look through old photographs.

Do not be scared to play old videos so that you might hear my voice and see me laughing.

Do not be wary of visiting my favourite places or eating my favourite foods or singing along to my favourite songs.

I know it will hurt. Those memories will remind you that I am gone.

They will stab at you like a knife in an open, gaping wound. Raw, excruciating pain.

But after a while the knife will become less sharp, the wound will become less open and the pain will become less raw.

And those memories will remind you that I was here.

That I lived.

Do not reduce my life to my death.

Speak my name, hear my voice, sing my favourite songs and visit my favourite places.

Because that's how I can stay alive a little.

Right here with you.

–Becky Hemsley

THE MEMORIAL TREE

Sleep came surprisingly easy that night. The weeks of crying and exhaustion had finally caught up with me. The funeral brought a sense of relief. I could finally say goodbye. I slept a solid eight hours and woke feeling like there was a light at the end of the very dark tunnel. I knew it was time to move on. I had no idea how that was possible but I owed it to myself and to my dad to move on. He would not want me to be sad and suffering. I had to find the path to my new future and I hoped he would still be guiding me.

"Let's go and see the flowers at the cemetery," Mum said. We all put on our coats and shoes and piled into Mark's car to visit the cemetery. The flowers were all laid in a long row on the pathway to the right of the chapel. We hadn't gotten the chance to see all the flowers at the funeral, so it was nice to see them and read all of the lovely messages. Mum asked us all to carry the flowers and place them under the memorial tree that Dad had chosen. We all carried the many floral tributes down the path to the tree whilst Mum disappeared inside the chapel. A short while later, she appeared. "Dad's ashes are ready," she said. None of us were expecting that so soon. She explained that the lady in the crematorium would bring them to us. In the distance, we saw her walking towards us carrying Dad's ashes in a box the size of a shoebox. Our dad was reduced to dust and ash in a small box. The lady knew Dad very well and passed on her condolences to us all. She passed the box to Mum, and we all stood there crying at Dad's tree. "Let's scatter his ashes," Mum said. Mark went to his car to retrieve some plastic disposable gloves that he had in his work box, stored in the boot of his car. He handed me, Mum and Hayley, a pair of gloves each. The three of

149

us dug a trench in the earth around the base of Dad's tree. Mum carefully lifted off the lid of the box and unfastened the bag that was sitting inside it. It was holding Dad safely inside. We all looked in and there was a greyish-white powder that glistened. One by one, we put our gloved hands into the box and took a handful of Dad's ashes. We carefully sprinkled him into the channel beneath his tree. We continued until the box was empty and the soil was covered over. All of us were sobbing uncontrollably. The task was complete and another of Dad's wishes could be ticked off the list in his little grey notebook.

Mark came to take the soiled gloves from us. Mum and Hayley handed them theirs, but I could not. I stood there crying, not able to give him the gloves. I gently peeled them off inside out and placed them in my pocket. They still had earth on them that glistened with particles of Dad's ashes. I could not throw them away. We all placed the flowers on top of the earth under the tree. It was time to go home.

We all arrived back at mums. We were all very pleased that the ashes had been ready that day. It meant that we had no time to prepare for it, to get upset before it. It happened with perfect timing. I had been through every stage and I would not have wanted to miss that. We did everything together as a family through the whole painful ordeal. It strengthened our bond and made our dad proud.

We sat in the garden together and Mum told us that it was time to sell the family home. I was gutted. Fifty-four years of making memories in our home and she wanted to sell it! "Just give it time, Mum," I said. I asked her to think long and hard about it, but her mind was made up. "I will take my memories with me," she said. She was right. The house was just a shell and not a home now that Dad was not part of it. It felt cold and empty. He had died in the house, it did not feel like our home anymore. Mum needed to forge a new life for herself. She had only known a life with Dad so it was not going to be easy. "I want to move to Hampshire with Hayley," she said. As painful as it was to think about strangers living in our home, it was the right thing to do. A new family making their own memories and we had to hope that they would love that house the way that we did.

I glanced over and spotted Dad's old blue canvas gardening shoes that were always placed by the conservatory entrance. "I have an idea, sis," I said. I went to get the shoes and asked Hayley to help me bury them. The shoes that had spent hours on Dad's feet whilst he worked away in his beloved garden. They were in tatters, but we could not throw them away. Hayley went to the shed to get a spade, and she dug a hole in the same spot where our Sausage Dog Cassie had been buried several years before. We placed the shoes in the hole and covered them over. The shoes are where they belong, in

Dad's garden forever.

We all spent the evening inside, talking together about our new future. We had a lot of preparations to make and made a list of things that we had to do before we could move on.

- SELL DAD'S CAR
- CONTACT THE PENSION COMPANY
- PUT THE HOUSE ON THE MARKET
- DONATE DAD'S BELONGINGS
- HELP MUM MOVE

The following day, Mark managed to get the car sold and I contacted different Estate Agents to get the house valued. Appointments were made for the valuations and with the Solicitor. We put the wheels in motion pretty quickly. Dad's pension was sorted and we helped Mum pack up her things. None of us could touch Dad's clothes and belongings. It was not the time for that. His room looked like a shrine, untouched, and we needed it to stay like that for the time being. His radio sat silently on his bedside table. His watches were stored safely in his closet and time had stood still in that room.

We chose an Estate Agent and the board went outside at the top of the steps. That was sad, but I knew it was for the best. Hayley would be looking after my mum, and I was grateful for that. I could not go back to Spain leaving my mum on her own. It was time for me to go home to Spain once again and Hayley and Mum back to Hampshire to wait for the family home to be sold. Keys were given to the agent and we locked the door to the house another time. We all made our way to our new lives and respective homes, knowing so much more had to be done. I felt empty on the plane journey home with Rob. He had missed me and I needed to find my way back to my old life, one day at a time.

THE NEW NORM

My life had to move forward. I felt trapped in the past, constantly reflecting on everything that had happened—the good, but mostly the bad. The constant vision of Dad's suffering was literally playing like a movie in my head. A once strong, independent man reduced to a frail wreck who depended on us literally for everything. To see him just wither away in front of my eyes was something I had to battle with, day in and day out. Sleepless nights laying awake for hours, begging for the ability to see good things in my mind's eye. I craved flashbacks to the good old days, our holidays, family times together and hearing Dad's many jokes. I knew things would never be the same again. How could they be?

Rob stayed constant, trying to understand

my pain and suffering. I could not articulate how I really felt inside, so instead, I plunged myself into my work. I communicated less and less, he struggled with the distance that I had put between us. I hoped he loved me enough to ride the storm with me. My once relentless inner strength had dwindled away to nothing. I was weak—a weakness borne from the constant flow of tears. The waves of sadness that washed over me daily were wreaking havoc with my mental and physical well-being. I was pushing everyone away, keeping a conscious distance between myself and my loved ones. I was so afraid of losing anyone else. I knew that if I had lost anyone else, it would have broken me. My walls were up, they were my defense mechanism. I had to find my way back.

The weeks went past in a flurry. Mum found a buyer for the family home. A lovely young family, just what I had hoped for. Hayley, Mark and I, but mostly Mark and Hayley, had the task of literally packing up everything in the home. Dad's clothes and belongings were all packed away and our uncle collected them to sort through. Dad and he had always swapped clothes, so it seemed right that now he got first pickings from his things. What he didn't want was delivered to the Cancer Research charity shop. All of Mum and Dad's worldly goods, bar a small box of trinkets and keepsakes, were packed up and also donated to the charity shop. We cleaned the house from top to bottom leaving it in a pristine condition, ready for the new owners to move in. I hope they make their own beautiful memories like we all did.

Mum's new life had now begun. She had her own newly decorated room at Hayley and Mark's house. She was surrounded by family and friends. This arrangement was perfect for her. She felt safe and I found comfort in knowing that she was not alone. The grief was showing on her face. She kept it all inside, one tough, strong cookie, my mum. She wasn't fooling me, though. I saw the emptiness in her eyes. She missed my dad terribly. We all collectively made sure that she was okay. She was our new priority.

The signs from Dad were coming thick and fast. A robin flew into our office in Spain and circled my desk before flying off. Our lights at home occasionally flash like disco lights... I could hear Dad in my mind, "Turn the lights off. It's like Blackpool illuminations." He was always very frugal at home with the lighting. Mum went to a spiritualist church, and Dad came through. The messages were just so detailed and we knew that Dad had found a way to let Mum know he was okay. He is waiting there for her. We know we will see him again. We have more memories to make.

With each day that passed, the grief became easier to deal with, still catching me off guard when I least expected it, but I developed a way of coping with it. Christmas was just around the corner and I just wasn't sure I wanted to celebrate it. The firsts of everything, I suppose, will always be the hardest. Dad loved Christmas, dragging us all around the garden centres to see the wonderful displays, the dancing reindeer, and freshly cut Christmas trees. He loved it all. He proudly decorated the Christmas tree every year that took pride of place in the bay window of the lounge. The tree was given to my lovely cousin and his wife. They sent me a photo of it in their home, standing proudly in their lounge.

I shed a few tears seeing it. He loved them just as they had loved him. The Christmas tree had found its new home. My flights were booked and off I went to see my family for a festive visit. I bought a beautiful display of winter greenery laced with pine cones, Holly and shiny red berries. My son and I went to the memorial tree to place the flowers there for him and we hung a Robin redbreast from the branches of his tree.

We spent a few moments in silence and walked away, leaving Dad behind us.

Mum found a new confidence and asked if we would go on a cruise with her, so now we all have something to look forward to. She had always wanted to go on a cruise, so of course, Hayley and I are going to go with her. I will be making those arrangements and one port of call will be Portofino. The gloves that are covered in the soil from the memory tree and sprinkled with Dad's glittery ashes will be going with us. I will rinse the remains of his ashes in the ocean there. Dad will fulfil his dream of going to Portofino. I knew I would get him there one day.

My new Norm is gradually taking shape. The tears still flow but I tell myself that this is because I had loved and had been loved so unconditionally. I was lucky to have the father that I had. A father that I still have because he is still with me. My memories of the pain and suffering that he had endured are becoming more blurred, and, instead, I now see colourful, beautiful memories that go back a whole lifetime. I was so lucky I got the chance to spend so much time with my dad at the end of his life. I got to tell him all the things I was grateful for, to tell him how loved he was and that I could not have wished for a better father. I had the luxury of being able to say goodbye. Not everyone gets that chance, so, ironically, and as painful as it all was, I was grateful to have had that time with him.

My dad had one purpose in life and that was to be a good husband and father. He excelled in both. He loved us all and provided for us well. He was instrumental in the making of so many wonderful memories. Memories that we could now all cling to. Memories to last a whole lifetime. He had a plan all along.

The boats are still bobbing on the river, the leaves still rustling in the tree at the bottom of the steps of our old family home. Dad is still surrounding us and sending his signs from time to time, but it's now time to set him free. His job is done.

ABOUT THE AUTHOR

Tracey Van Deer was born in the south west of England. She is a mother of three and grandmother to four, living in Spain with her Dutch husband, Rob. Together, they run a successful Estate Agency. Although work keeps her very busy, Tracey has found time to finally fulfill her dream of writing a book.

The nagging voice from her Literature teacher in the '70s stayed firmly in her head for many moons. "You must write, Tracey." Fast forward to 2024, and her first book was born: a heartbreaking memoir about the saddest time of her life, written with eyes blurred from tears. The copious amount of biscuits and cups of tea consumed did offer some comfort.